# HAPPILY EVER AFTER

THAYIL EDITIONS

*Soliloquies* | Adil Jussawalla

*My Dead Flowers* | Buku Sarkar

FORTHCOMING

*Let the Smithereens* | Karthika Naïr

*damn you / a magazine of the arts:* Facsimile Edition | Edited by Alok Rai, Arvind Krishna Mehrotra, Amit Rai

*You've Come to the Right Place* | Joshua Muyiwa

## PRAISE FOR *HAPPILY EVER AFTER*

'Kamal Trilok Singh's *happily ever after* reads like a long close-up, the Bergman kind, with the searing rage of Chantal Akerman. This isn't a romance; it's a visceral autopsy performed at Bar-Bar over a drink that's mostly ice and regret. It marks the arrival of a writer who trusts the power of stillness—and knows exactly when to break it. "Love is just a well-poured glass of Old Monk, and I am supposed to knock it down like a dumb bitch." Welcome to Delhi—once upon a time my city—which in Singh's writing "stinks of petrol and slaughtered dreams". In the marriage detailed in this book, there are no grand betrayals, no operatic collapses. Nothing explodes. Things erode. A gesture withheld. A joke that lands wrong. A plant left unwatered. Moment by moment, the self thins. The novel's power comes from its claustrophobic interiority, much like Akerman's *Jeanne Dielman*. It's the voice of someone who sees too much and cannot unknow it. A mind circling the same wounds, trying to locate the exact moment where love turned into performance. This is a world where a brass bell is used to signal the end of domestic combat, where “scheduled intimacy” feels like “necrophilia with better lighting” and where faking an orgasm is less about pleasure and more about “evidence that we’re still here”. What struck me most is the control beneath the fury. The repetitions, the erotic charge, the domestic details—all of it accumulates with precision. The narrator’s voice is ferocious, vulnerable and unsparing—especially towards herself. She is not asking to be absolved. She is asking to be seen. Unsettling, precise and emotionally fearless, *happily ever after* announces a writer who knows that the real drama is not in the Great Indian Wedding—but in what survives it.’

**Dev Benegal**

‘Every page in this book makes one thing clear: Kamal Trilok Singh’s characters are not okay, and he’s about to make every single one of us pay for it. Because neither are we. Here is a book you can smell. Smoke, flesh, rot and routine carry a particularly sharp odour in Singh’s writing. Scents that don’t evaporate easily when you put his story away. You will want to look elsewhere, and then you won’t, because the author is generous enough to make his terrifying clarity everyone else’s problem.

You will feel sick and satiated in equal measure, which is likely exactly what he intends. Singh confronts the death of forever, the death of desire, the slow death of the little lies we tell ourselves to maintain some sense of order. They accumulate like paper cuts until there's no blood left to lose. Singh's most impressive achievement, however, is in locating true brutality in the everyday violences we inflict upon ourselves. There is sex, shame and flashes of liberation; reckoning, reflection and an uneasy sense of silent suffering. You don't need to have lived this story to be marked by it. Though the truth is that too many of us have. In the end, it feels less like fiction and more like an implication. An open challenge to the impossible weight of the gendered expectations we carry. How much have we survived by looking away, and how deep are the cracks when we're forced to reckon with our own choices? Somewhere between catharsis and a curse, *happily ever after* is a scathing indictment of the love stories we've been sold, and it is Kamal Trilok Singh's attempt to break those shackles.'

**Mandovi Menon**

# HAPPILY EVER AFTER

**KAMAL TRILOK SINGH**

FOURTH ESTATE · *New Delhi*

First published in India by Fourth Estate 2026
An imprint of HarperCollins *Publishers*
By arrangement with Thayil Ink
HarperCollins *Publishers* India, Cyber City,
Building 10-A, Gurugram, Haryana – 122002, India
www.harpercollins.co.in

2 4 6 8 10 9 7 5 3 1



P-ISBN: 978-93-6989-268-6
E-ISBN: 978-93-6989-317-1



Typeset in 11/15.5 Aldine401 BT at
HarperCollins *Publishers* India

Printed and bound in India by
Manipal Technologies Limited

MIX
Paper | Supporting responsible forestry
FSC™ C043100

This book is produced from independently certified FSC® paper to ensure responsible forest management.

HarperCollins *Publishers*, Macken House, 39/40 Mayor Street Upper,
Dublin 1, D01 C9W8, Ireland

I was at a bar. Not drinking. Not really. Just sitting there, existing in that low hum where the world felt like skin I could peel off, head buzzing with Kishore, in my father's voice, soft and off-key, celluloid, from back when the days didn't feel like an ambush. And I smiled (I think), wondering if I'd left the geyser on, fuck it, and I thought about my little habit then, the one that makes me feel rotten, of sketching the faces of men I want to ruin. Faces pulled out of the muck; loose-jawed, shifty-eyed, unremarkable assholes who wouldn't hold my gaze if I stapled their eyelids open. I'd draw them quick, a flash, dirty, fast, mean lines, angles I dreamt of crushing under my thumb, the cartilage popping, wet and satisfying. The lips I'd chew into liquidy rust, blood warm in my mouth, until their teeth went soft under my tongue. The throats I'd drive into piss and prayer. Sometimes, I'd add details the world didn't offer. A cheek sagging open like split fruit. A jaw hanging dumb and broken. Eyes gone fish-dead, slick but stupid. My sketches. My drafts. My dry run. Not a fantasy. Foreplay. A violence I could fold and carry in my pocket. A thing to take out in bathrooms, and lick to climax. Then flush it; the face the man the mess.

Gone.

*On my fifth drink, or maybe the sixth.* I don't know I don't know I don't know. But it is nice, the not knowing. And who gives a shit? The blur is part of the charm. Oblivion has a nice curve to it when you're wearing heels and a grudge. And somewhere between sips, I check his profile. Of the one who said he loved me. Wrote it like a prayer in my inbox, trembling-spilling himself. Weeks later, he was still posting songs about me, all lowercase, all pathetic. I scroll through his scrapbook life: the wife, happy, the dog, the Sunday sunlight on a balcony, curated green; and it makes me feel sharp and alive. It makes me want to throw up.

We had plants too. You remember? You'd been the one who got me excited; insisted, made me pick the pots, and promised you'd water them. You didn't. You never did. After the first week, they were mine: my duty, my guilt. Every time I'd drag the watering can, I'd stare at the cracked soil and imagine it was the soft spot at the back of a skull; and I'd press down until it gave. Watch the dirt spill, clumped and dry, just to see if I'd feel anything about killing something you promised to keep alive. At times, I wanted them dead. I wanted the slow rot to be deliberate. A lesson.

They're gone now, the plants. The balcony is bare, a strip of sun, dust and concrete. Sometimes I stand there and draw faces I want to ruin, slack mouths and coward eyes, cutting them open in my head, a red spill, gut and shit, while they're inside me. And when I come, it's not about them. It's not about the fuck or the face or the blood. It's about me. It's proof that I am. And I don't apologize for it any more.

*Old Monk*, you declared on our first date. *You can have as much as you want without worrying about the bill.* I laughed at your audacity. Not because it was funny, but because you were already mine, already naked; shameless, like a dog that's been kicked too many times, and still crawls back when called. And I thought, fuck this boy, I love him I love him I love him the way a cat loves a cornered mouse; tenderly, and with patience. I loved you for your apologetic sadness, the kind that begged permission to exist. I also hated you for it, for how much it reminded me of my own sadness.

Later, we fucked. Of course we did. And I loved it. You were different. Like someone trying to scrub a stain from inside their ribs. Like your cock was a voice, and each thrust a confession, absurd; your moans an apology long overdue. I let you slap me, not hard, not cruel, just enough to see if I'd flinch, enough to know we were both watching. I didn't flinch. *Try harder.* You needed that. I needed worse. And then you came like a secret too loaded to carry, and I let you blast it on my face. I wanted to see if you'd say sorry. You didn't. You never did. And in the silence after, I realized I didn't want you to.

The love. It hit me like a speeding truck—bang—smacked goddamn bone-first, shattering the part of me that still believed in soft landings. It was the way you poured our drinks, head bowed, hands trembling like a junkie savouring the ritual, treating that dark piss-water with holy reverence, ice cubes clicking like broken teeth, worshipping the glass because it never asked questions, never asked for anything. It was pathetic. It was holy. The ritual meaningless—made meaningful by your devotion to it. I almost laughed. I almost kissed you for it. I should've known then. You were a priest. You were an addict. You were a coward too. You made suffering look sacred. And maybe that's the part I can't forgive myself for: that I loved you more for it. That I wanted to take your cowardly devotion, and tuck it warm in my cunt, where the soft animal of you could finally stop trembling.

And I searched your face for hints of what festered underneath. The lines dim on your forehead told me more than your words ever did. Beneath your demeanour was calm deception you wore like a mask. Practised and bathroom-rehearsed. That sacred little stage where you'd stare into yourself, palms flat against the sink, as if it were the only thing keeping you from collapse. The mirror?

Forgiving. Complicit. It was a calm curated, bullshit—the kind men wear to avoid becoming headlines.

Sometimes I'd stand barefoot in the dark hallway, shoulder pressed to the wall, watching you in the bathroom mirror. Arms rigid. Elbows locked. Spine stiff. You'd stare at yourself. Not with vanity, but with dread, as if you were bracing for something; your fingers tracing the reflection like it might disappear if you blinked. I swear, sometimes I thought you were trying to *touch* your soul and found the glass in the way. Then came the ritual: a thumb dragged across each brow, creasing the line. Next, you'd jerk your neck, left-right until it went *krickth*. I'd watch your jaw tighten—then release—then tighten again; your bones negotiating the terms of existence. You'd inhale, too slow too deep, a pause too long, as if to breathe were sin and confession wrapped into one. I told myself I didn't pity you. Or maybe I did. Maybe I pitied myself more, standing there, waiting, hoping you'd look up. You never did. Gravity is harder for men pretending not to fall apart. Next, you'd drop your voice. Tune it to casual and test a few words. *Hey. I'm good. Yeah, not bad, fine fine fucking fine.* You'd say it like prayer like spell; like you could chant yourself into being okay. Then you'd smile, rehearsed tight, tragic; and I'd watch from the shadows, throat knotted in knowing, wondering what it meant that you never once saw me, and why I kept standing there anyway.

Sometimes I got bored. So, I'd slip past the doorway and step before the mirror, blocking your reflection. I'd tilt my head and grin at you, teeth bared, like a dare: Kiss me or kill me. You never did either. Once, I even spat on the mirror, a wet streak over your careful mask, and whispered, *now you've got the uglies too*. You wiped it off without looking at me. I think I liked that, being the smudge on your sermon, the chaos in your mirror.

The days were worse. The sun came through the blinds in little prison stripes. I'd lie on the floor, cheek to cold tile, listening to the neighbours vacuuming, frying eggs, laughing—whole lives moving around me like fish behind glass. One morning, I yanked the blinds open all the way.

Let the light flood the room until it stabbed your eyes. You groaned. I felt triumphant. Another time, I wrapped your belt around my neck, tight, just to see the mark it left. A red ring, like a bruise that pointed fingers. You said nothing. I laughed into the cushion till I coughed on dust. Then, this one time, I took your toothbrush and scraped the inside of the toilet with it. Rinsed it. Put it back. Watched you brush your teeth that night, a private performance for me. When you kissed me later, I thought, *now you're mine in a way you'll never know*.

The nights were quieter. I'd sit at the kitchen table, retro songs on repeat, father in memory, gnawing the inside of my cheek until it bled, imagining what the world would look like without me in it. Not in some poetic way. Just curiosity. I called you, once, while you were asleep in the next room. I wanted to hear my name in your voice, the soft, irritated *what?* You answered, and I didn't speak. I just breathed. You said my name twice, and for that moment, I was a god. Then you hung up. I wasn't waiting for you to save me. I was watching to see if you'd notice I was gone before I ever left.

The performance of stillness. It never fit quite right. It looked borrowed on you; worn in, but passable. You'd mastered the cues; how to nod-smile, say I'm fine I'm fine I'm fine without a tremor or a twitch. And you said it like it meant something. Like it was earned. Because you knew; one slip, one sigh too long, one blink too heavy, and it would all fall apart—the raw, the rot, the too-much. So, you performed. Every day. Every mirror. Tugging your skin into something legible. Until the mask held. Until you could walk out and say *morning* like the silence in your chest wasn't growing teeth.

And I?

I think what broke me wasn't your silence. It was that I was waiting for it to end. That is what ruined me: hope dressed as patience. I waited. Because I believed that after all those mornings of watching you rehearse yourself into something passable, you'd eventually turn, look at me, say my name, and show me what lived beneath. But you never did. You just kept polishing that mask like an heirloom, like it was your only inheritance. As if letting it slip even once might drown the whole goddamn room. And maybe it would. Maybe it should. And maybe I was afraid of that, too. Because if it came to it, I'd have to choose between saving myself and saving us.

Like that one evening, when you were chopping onions. Just that. Nothing tragic. A Tuesday. You looked up, eyes wet from the sting, and I joked, *you crying?* You laughed. Not really. More a spasm behind the teeth. Then: I used to cry a lot as a kid, you said. Still looking down. Still slicing. And I stilled everything, my hands, my breath. Held open the silence, an invitation: *Come lie down inside me. Say more. Tell me where it hurt. Show me who made you swallow your tears.* But you didn't tell me more. The oil bubbled. You chopped. The onions sizzled. And that was it. You never said why. Never said when. Never gave me the shape of the boy who used to cry. I would've loved that boy, awkward and snot-nosed, elbows and ache, whatever he was. Would've built him a nest inside my ribs. Would've asked about the monsters, and sung him a lullaby. But you didn't let me. You gave me a shard, then acted like it was the whole mirror. And I held it, telling myself, maybe—just maybe—you were trying. But you weren't.

I hated you for that, and not in the way you'd expect, the petty storming-out fuck-you kind of hate. No. Mine was an infection: slow, curling in the wet heat of my panties, untouched, on nights you said, *not tonight*. It lived there, festering, a patient parasite feeding on the quiet of being unseen. Because I gave you *everything*. I cracked open the whole damn mess—the bile, the ache, the shame-stained stories. All of it.

And you?

You watched, detached polite, as if we were an anecdote for dinner parties.

Yes, I told you everything. More than memory, I gave you evidence. Told you about pissing myself in fifth grade and sitting through math soaked in shame. Told you about the uncle who came in after the lights were out. Told you about hiding in the wardrobe with my hands between my legs, shielding *it*, because my tiny fucking hands, weak hands, were the only thing I could protect myself with. Told you about summers hiding cigarette burns under long sleeves. Told you about the teacher with soft hands and a sugar voice, who followed me into the bathroom, and whispered that I was brilliant, and I could stay brilliant, his favourite, if I kept my mouth shut. So, I did. Told you about the day my best friend decided I wasn't her best friend any more, how she passed me in the corridor holding someone else's hand, laughing the way we used to. Told you about my cousin who found my garden stash—a box of notes, bottle caps and little stolen things I thought were treasures. She showed everyone, and they laughed. I never hid anything again. Told you about walking home at midnight, praying to gods I didn't believe in. Told you about the breakdown in the mall parking lot when a toddler screamed like I used to. Told you about the rope, the bedsheet, the knot—just in case. Told you about my mother's hatred, and how her face wilted every time I smiled. The way her eyes snagged on my perky tits like they were mocking her. No slaps. No screams. Just a sigh, deep, not tired, but resentful. When I walked past in a towel, she'd pretend not to look, but her neck twitched, and her jaw set in that way it did when she thought life had cheated her. She hated my skin. My glow. My gait. The ease with which men followed me. Not because it made me powerful, but because it reminded her of everything she once was and would never be again. And she spoke to me only to correct. Only to say: *Why are you like this? Have some shame. Put on some clothes.* As if I were a betrayal of her womb; as if I had been spat out just to humiliate her. And the cruellest part? I didn't fight it. I obeyed. Folded. Stayed small. Walked soft. Laughed less. Covered up. Made myself a daughter she could almost love, but never quite. Because nothing in me would ever be old enough to make her feel young again.

See. I gave it all. *Everything.* Even the parts that stank. The shame-soaked touch sessions where I cried and came at the same time, trying to feel something that wasn't rot. Even that. And you held me like an object that might fall apart if you pressed too hard. So, you never pressed. You just … hovered … a ghost with good intentions.

And I?

I was the girl who kissed you in bathrooms, balconies and rickshaws, trying to feel something *real*, scrape meaning out of heat. And we were both faking it. Your hands moved without curiosity, sliding like you were following a map. You cupped my breasts, as if checking for weight, not want, and the touch felt clinical. And you said nothing when I moaned too soon too loud, when all of it felt like a parody. And in that moment, with your body in mine, I thought of Ma, folding towels with surgical precision. She never let me help. Said I got the folds wrong, ruined the corners. Said neatness was a woman's duty. So, I stayed neat, folded like those towels, quiet-manageable, rocking back and forth while your eyes drifted past my face, past the bedroom, past even the moment; and I stared at the fan, the thin coat of dust on blades, thinking, I should clean that. Then, I remembered the first time you said I was beautiful. Drunk, in the stairwell, your breath fogging the air between us. Like a joke. I laughed like I believed it. And now, here I was, face twitching with effort, trying not to drift out of my body, holding on, while your hands squeezed the meat of me. I wanted to cry, but I didn't. I just whispered, voice cracked, *can I come?* And you said, *hmm.* Like my wanting was a minor inconvenience. A gnat, with a static buzz. And that was the kill shot. Not the silence. Not the mask. But the *hmm.* So, fuck that, fuck you. And fuck us.

You never loved me. You took notes, hoping for a good metaphor someday.

Here is a metaphor for you: *Sluts burn like old books—every page ash, every silence a scream.*

A friend once told me to leave you. Said it flat: *Divorce him. Save yourself.* I laughed in her face. Played the loyal idiot.

Told her she didn't get what we had. We fought in her kitchen, my voice breaking each time I offered a defence I didn't believe. I swore I'd never speak to her again, and I kept that promise. That night, I told you what she said. And I wanted fire. I wanted you to grab me, to swear I was worth the fight, to rage at the idea of losing me. Instead, you just nodded. Said, *she's not wrong you know*, like you were talking about the fucking weather. I laughed, changed the subject, pretending it didn't gut me open. I miss her now. Some nights, I think of her chopping coriander, with that look on her face, *you'll regret this*. I grabbed my phone, and WhatsApped her. *Hey. Remember me?*

Sometimes you cried with me. Not really. Not *tears* in the way that mean anything. Not grief that stutters breath. Yours were tiny bursts. Controlled. Self-aware. A glisten at the edges. A clenched fist. And a silence that went on so long it sagged. One time, your voice cracked, trembled, and you whispered, *it'll be fine it'll be fine it'll be fine,* like a prayer scratched on a bathroom wall.

And fuck me. Because I believed it. And I let it settle in my chest, hoping it might hold me up for a while.

And you?

Maybe you thought it was enough, a cracked whisper masquerading as love.

Later, the shame came in waves. *Chutiya saali, dumb bitch dumb bitch dumb bitch*, I muttered, and slap slap slapped myself quiet.

*Stop it. You're in a bar*, I reminded myself. *Among strangers. Smile. Look normal.*

*On my fifth drink, or maybe the sixth*. I don't know I don't know I don't know. But it was nice, the not knowing, and the glass sweating in my hand, the low hum of other people's lives around me; all of it softening the edges for a little while.

You told me once you got beat up at boarding school. That was it. Your entire boyhood flattened into one antiseptic line, a single offering. And I took it. Held it as though it were fragile, convinced it was the key to loving you right, a secret I could cradle into meaning.

But it wasn't enough. I knew. You knew, too. It was scaffolding; cowardice dressed as composure. You called it maturity. I called it bullshit, *camouflage.*

And I lived under this scaffolding for a decade. Fed it. Fucked it. Convinced myself it was love. I wrote poems. Sketched faces. Metabolized grief. I rearranged my life around your absence and called it warmth.

There is a special kind of death in being seen, but never met. You watched me tear myself open, devout, as if each confession were an act I owed you. And you never once flinched at the pain. Of course not. Pain's quiet. Abstract. It doesn't stain your shirt. You can pretend not to notice it. But you flinched at the *mess*—the inconvenience and the fucking tears. You wanted a performance without the person. The drama without the gore. A tragedy in clean lighting, a crying woman who *knew how to mop up after herself.*

So, I obliged. Learnt to bleed neat. No stains. No sound. Just enough damage to feel poetic, but not enough to make you stay up at night. I was the comfortable ache you could bandage and parade as proof of your goodness. And I let you. I let myself shrink into the version of a *wreck* you could hold without effort.

*Crying, version 1:* I learnt in stairwells. Out the door, mid-cigarette mid-night. I'd feel it coming, the ache, the spiral, and I'd excuse myself. Just getting some air, I'd mutter, waiting for it, standing outside in the dark, coatless, bare arms in buzzy cold, watching the neighbours' TVs flicker through their windows—sitcoms and game shows, tiny warm lies I wasn't invited into. And I'd cry quietly, neatly, with a dignified face, chin tipped up just enough for the tears to land clean, without leaving a trace. Behind the potted ficus someone left for dead—I finally matched the damn thing.

*Crying, version 2:* I'd touch up the concealer before crying. Raw-eyed in the bathroom mirror, tap-tapping the sponge like a prayer; like maybe if I could soften the reflection, the emptiness might shut up. I'd check the mirror twice, once for symmetry, once for sanity. Make sure the puffiness looked poetic, pretty-tragic. Not unhinged. Not wild. Not *mad*. Blot the tears, careful, like grease off a dosa—soft-soft quick-quick. Can't have you seeing it. Would ruin the night, the vibe. And then came the hair, lipstick redone, hem tugged into place, smile pinched on like a bandage. Because you'd made reservations. Texted me. Wear the black dress. The one that makes your collarbones look like knives. And my stomach twisted so hard I thought I'd puke. But I didn't. Instead, I powdered the sweat above my lip, swallowed the bile, stood barefoot on cold tiles and whispered: *Don't ruin this for him don't ruin this for him don't ruin this for him.*

And fuck me, I hated that my first thought was still you. Hated how my body flinched at the idea of your hand sliding up my thigh under white linen napkins, edging close to the panties. And still: I tied the hair back, sprayed perfume behind each ear, dabbed gloss on my mouth, and stepped out into the night. A bruise covered in silk. And you looked at me and said, *you look nice*. And

I smiled, and we kissed. Because that was the deal. I bring the tragedy. You: the reservation.

*Crying, version 3:* I cried during the rinse cycle. Washer spinning like a drunk. On repeat. Violent, predictable. Sat on the kitchen tile, back against the counter, next to the detergent bottle because its lemon scent reminded me of women who seemed to have their lives together, who didn't cry in stairwells or bathrooms—all, while also thinking of the designs I hadn't filed, the boss who still thought I was reliable, and a colleague's unread message I couldn't bear to answer, her optimism too much for my kind of day. It wasn't anything dramatic that set me off. Just your shirt. Cotton, pale blue, collar frayed. I should have thrown it out. Instead, I washed it. Watched through the tempered glass, fabric twisting-choking, then floating again, hypnotic. Almost gentle if I ignored the roar of the spin.

Funny how grief finds you in stupid places. Not at gravesides, not under moonlight, but here, on cracked tile, while there's detergent on your fingers, and you're feeling small and invisible.

Forty minutes. Cotton. Thirty degrees.

The machine hummed its low, steady prayer, promising softness, brightness, a return to new. But nothing comes out new. Just wet. Small. Smaller. Shrunken by heat and time and too much spinning.

I sat there, crying into the lemon scent, thinking of all that I'd washed away. The wine stain from that night you raised your voice. The kohl blot on the pillow sleeves. The blood from the morning I wasn't sure I'd make it out of bed. And load after load, the machine took it all. No questions. No judgement. And I thought: Maybe that's what I want love to be. Just something that cleans without asking where the stains came from, or why they keep coming back.

And then, one night: driving back from dinner. Nothing fight-worthy. Just rain, warm and greasy on the windshield. At the red light, we saw it—a tree, a big, old, proud bastard uprooted, rain sluicing through it, roots twitching like veins that didn't know they were done. And in that moment, it didn't look like a thing of wood. It looked like a body, ribs cracked, belly spilling its quiet rot on to the road. And I swear, for a second, it turned its wet ruined face to me and said something only I could hear: *Look, sweetheart, even the things that hold on the longest come undone.* And I felt it. Not pity. But recognition. A cold animal knowing in my chest. Because it wasn't just a tree, it was *me*, laid bare in grainy red, all things hidden, now showing. And you exhaled and said, *guess it was time.*

You didn't look at me. Didn't clock the way my hands curled into fists. Didn't see the wild, stupid ache your words kicked up. Because fuck … that tree had stood longer than either of us had been alive. And it still fell. No warning. No spectacle. And you, with your practised calm, shrugged, said, *guess it was time.*

And I knew then, that you'd say the same about me. If I fell. If I snapped. You'd shrug. Maybe flinch at the *mess,* glance in the rearview, but you'd keep driving. You always keep driving.

So, when we pulled into our street, I opened the door before the engine died. *I'll walk*, I said. Not loud. Not angry. Just enough for you to hear. And I shut the door on whatever you did or didn't say.

I got home, rain-wet, mascara stiff on my lashes, and I did it. Wrote the damn note on WhatsApp. Typed it slow. Read it three times. Hit send. Saw the double tick, panicked and deleted it. Gone. And you, reeking of dinner wine and useless composure, asked, *what was that … that thing you sent and deleted?*

*Nothing, just a dumb video*, I said, and smiled at my screen, like a girl pretending she'd sent the wrong meme, my heart hammering fists behind my ribs. Because what else could I say? That I almost bowed out mid-scroll? That the note was real, but death was inconvenient? That all it took to bring me there was a fallen tree and a man who could look at ruin and call it *timely*.

Later, in bed, I stared at the ceiling fan, dust thick on the blades. You slept easy, back turned, that soft little wheeze in your breath like someone who's never had to scream. And I thought about the tree, the roots twitching in the rain, still reaching for something, even after the ground said *no more*. And I didn't cry. Not that night. Just lay there and let that knowing settle in my bones.

I thought: One day, I'll fall, and you'll survive me; and you'll shrug eat drive fuck repeat. And maybe the only mercy I can give myself is this: That when I go—if I go—it won't be for you. It'll be for me. A clean ending. Quiet. No double ticks. No deleted notes. Just a body choosing stillness after all that spinning.

Later that night, later-later, I walked to the fridge. Not for food. Just for the cold. Just to feel something uninvited on my face. And I stood there, hand resting on the door, letting the hum crawl up my arm. Everything in that light looked staged. Curated. I grabbed the last egg and held it a moment, unsure, and then dropped it on the floor, a soft private splat, yolk blooming like an infection. I left it there. Closed the fridge, killed the light, went back to bed. Not angry. Not heroic. Just done.

Tomorrow I'll buy six more, and line them up like teeth. A quiet truth I won't have to explain.

The next morning, I walked back to the spot. Just to be sure it had really happened. And there it was, or what was left of it. The tree. My stubborn, *fallen* goddamn metaphor. Men in neon vests buzzed around with chainsaws snarling, blades biting into what was once trunk, now carcass. Limbs hacked off, one by one, methodical, bored. Bark stripped. Guts exposed. A dull thud each time a piece hit the tar. No ceremony. No pause. The world, as always, in a rush to forget what it couldn't hold. A man looked at me, like, *you knew this tree?* I didn't nod. Just stood there in last night's jeans, stinking of sleep and something less essential to survival, witnessing the clean-up of this collapse, of something that had held up for decades and was gone overnight, chopped and hauled like it never mattered.

Then, I lit a cigarette I didn't want. Tasted ash. Felt the sting, and thought: *This is how the world forgets. Not with grief. But with protocol and logistics.*

By the time I got back, you were gone. The yolk from the previous night was still there. Dried. Crusted over. A line of ants had begun their march. I stepped over it, not with care, but calculation, a private dare to see how long I could coexist with the rot. Then, I opened the window. Let the smog claw in. I needed the room to know I was still here, still alive.

You were a liar, and god help me, I loved you for it. I knew that the first night, on that first date, when your mouth was deciding, still, whether to tell the truth or perform it. You chose performance. You always did. The careful way you say *it's fine* with your back turned, so I can never see the truth leaking from your eyes. But I forgave it, because your lies weren't cruel. They were the kind kids tell. I know. Because I lie too. Not with words that deceive, but with silence in the right places. I lie with wet thighs, a back arched and a welcome I don't feel. I lie with my steady hands guiding your hunger into me, even as my gut twists.

I lie with stillness, and the brittle calm I wear like Sunday linen. I lie with my tongue, whispering *yes yes yes*, while the rest of me screams, *get out get out get out*! I lie with the blade on my wrist, testing skin, saying out loud to no one, *I'm fine I'm fine I'm fine*. I lie with my cunt too: slick, willing, playing the part. And I lie with my hands firm on your hips, even as my insides knot, whispering in some back alley of myself: *Make him stay, make it count, make his body worth the space it takes, before he finishes and forgets your name.*

Because if I don't, you'll leave.

So, I lie the way I fuck. Just enough to be wanted. I moan on cue, sweet as flies on meat. And I let you blast it on my face and pretend it's a blessing.

These aren't the kind of lies that smash glass. These are *survival lies.* Soggy, harmless things folded into the day like socks in a drawer. These lies, they don't yell. But slowly, they rust you; they've rusted us.

They've made your voice taste of metal.

Like, when we lie in bed *not touching,* pretending that we aren't lonely. The way you kiss my forehead, careful, as if

I am a fever you don't want to catch. These lies don't bite. They seep, like mould, like piss; and from far away, they look like love. The kind Mary Oliver might've mistaken for hope if she hadn't watched the wild geese leave, and leave, and leave, and never return. These lies, they sit at breakfast, make the bed, cook dinner, tuck us in; and then, slip their hands around our necks while we sleep through a marriage we were too gutless to quit.

And they don't leave. They never fucking leave. They hold my hand while my cunt shrivels, swallowing the dust of my want. And they fold laundry while I fantasize about choking on your undies, not for arousal, but to see if I'd still gag.

And the worst part? They stop feeling like lies. They become the room. The air. The furniture. The wallpaper of our *us-ness.* Just silence. Just stillness. Just this fucking life dressed up like truth.

It was all there that first night. I saw it. The curl of your mouth around a joke you didn't finish. A half-laugh lodged in your throat. The pause before you let me in. Charm put forward as accident, muscle memory as spontaneity. The way your fingers gripped the glass too tight, like it might run. The ring of sweat left behind. You were quiet. But it wasn't mystery. It was staging. Your silence said more than your mouth ever would, *cautious,* waiting to see which version of you would survive the night, survive me. I know. Because I'd have done the same. If I could. But I couldn't. I've never been capable of performance. I was easy. Too easy. My mother had a word for it. *Slut.* She spat it out like holy water, hoping it would scrub me clean.

And still, I stayed. And I fucked. I cooked. Cleaned around the edges. Gathered crumbs for crows. Called it care. Called it *home.* Believed in it. Called it real. Called it us. Because what else was there. Because why not.

Ten years later. Tonight. I'm at Bar-Bar. *On my fifth drink, or maybe the sixth.* Who knows. Who gives a fuck. And I stare into the bottom of my glass for one clean memory. Maybe it remembers something I don't. I think of you pouring drinks on that first date, so careful, like it mattered, like you already knew how to perform tenderness, auditioning for the part of a man who could hold me without dropping me. Maybe love is just a well-poured glass of Old Monk, and I am supposed to knock it down like a dumb bitch. And I did. Expected salvation. Got shit. And now here I am, ten years and one wasted woman later, licking the rim of a glass, hoping for closure. But it's just ice. Silence in a different shape.

And I think, *goddamn, we grow up quick*. How quiet it is, the moment something breaks, and we call it becoming; and how we dry out like riverbeds, and still set the table on cracked earth, and pretend the dust on our tongues is love; and our lies, we pass down like family recipes. Life shifts. One moment, here we are. The next, we are history. A decade stitched up in silences—the what-if what-now and what-next.

I *imagine* the future sometimes. Years slow and beige. A soft death. Functional like furniture. Nothing dramatic. No heartbreak. No blood. Just us. Older. Still here. You at the dining table, scrolling on your phone, liking things you don't really like. Me, by the sink, rinsing the same plate, just for something to do with my hands. There's music on. A Spotify algorithm built from our silences. We don't speak, not because we're angry, but because there's nothing left to say that hasn't already been said in the scrape of a chair, the sighs, the hiss of the kettle, and the pause where touch used to live.

And there's a kid, maybe. Some hybrid of us, *fucked up*, with your stubborn mouth and my tired eyes. They draw something. Bring it over, ask, *is it good?* We nod. Lie like pros.

The plants on the balcony wilt. We don't talk about it. We just let them go. They used to hold promise—colourful pots lined up along the railing—basil, bougainvillea and a stubborn little aloe. And for a few weeks, we watered them religiously, morning and evening, as if tending to them might save us. You'd smile, press the soil with your finger to check the dampness, and call it *optimally moist*. Then, one afternoon, at the mall, I watched you hold a door open for a stranger, some woman with expensive scent and a careless smile. You never did that for me. Later, in the parking lot, I didn't take your hand when you reached for mine. You didn't ask why. We drove home, the silence humming, and something in me tilted. It has always been like this—not fight or flight, but a tiny unremarkable moment where the air changes, and never changes back. The next morning, you didn't show up to water the plants. Defiant, I didn't water them either. And that was it. The leaves yellowed, curled, went brittle against the heat, and we ignored it, until it was too ugly to look at. So, we assigned a Sunday for clean-up. Pulled out the roots, dragged the dead stems to the trash, wiped our hands on old newspaper and called it closure. Then, we bought new plants. Told ourselves this time would be different. This time we'd pay attention, give them the care they deserved. And every time, hope bloomed just long enough to rot.

I stop wearing earrings. Soon the lobe holes close. You don't notice. I used to wear gold hoops. You once told me I looked like trouble in them. Now, I could shave my head and bleed from the eyes, and you'd still ask if we're out of toothpaste. I stop painting my nails too. The bottles dry out where I left them, colours with names like *Desire*, *Barely*, *Heatwave.* Now my nails are short, blunt, the hands of someone who only touches dishes and grief. You don't notice that either.

Me? I see everything. The new grey by your temple. The crease between your brows. The cut on your finger you didn't tell me about. I notice how you shave in silence. How you sometimes hum when you think I'm not listening. The way your back has begun to stoop. How your breath catches when you sit down too fast. The way your belly folds when you tie your laces. I notice all of it. But I say nothing. Because once, when I said, *you look tired*, you flinched. I learnt to watch. Like a wife. Like a ghost. Like a voyeur in my own house.

There's a bookshelf we never touch. Dust gathers. We used to read. Now we stream shows we've already seen. Sex becomes a courtesy. Once a month, maybe. A polite fuck, like topping off someone's drink. I come out of memory.

You, as though rehearsed. We wipe up in silence. Then I sit on the cold toilet, panties around my knees, feeling a hollow that even crying can't reach. Birthdays shrink. Gifts become envelopes with vouchers. Cards left unsigned. You forget my favourite colour. I forget yours. The kid grows up. Learns not to knock. Keeps headphones on during dinner. Starts dating someone who looks nothing like either of us. Good.

I watch your hands. They don't look cruel. Just foreign.

One day, I pick your razor. Use it to shave my legs. Sit on the toilet lid afterwards and watch the faint red lines bloom where I nicked myself. I think maybe this is what dying really feels like—not pain, just vacancy.

We celebrate twenty years. Go out to eat. Toast to endurance. I wear a dress I hate. You say I look nice. I smile. Later, you go to bed first. Pretend to be asleep before I enter. I undress in the dark, peel off my bra. Lie beside you. Still. Not touching. Count the seconds, like a metronome, between our breaths. Convince myself we're in sync. Think: *This is it this is it this is it.* I don't know whether to laugh. Eventually, even ghosts get tired of haunting spaces and settle into the walls.

Tomorrow, we'll make coffee. We'll make toast. We'll say *morning* like it's a punctuation mark. And this—this soft beige death dressed as routine—will be our happily ever after.

I remember the first time I noticed how lonely your back looked in bed. Not sad. Just blank. You lay there like something abandoned—all shoulders and silence, the flat geometry of a body.

And still, I stayed. I wrapped my limbs around you. I loved. I fucked. I waited for the collapse. But the sob never came. You held it between your teeth: tight, bloodless, precise. I kissed you anyway, pressed my mouth to yours, wanting to suck it out of you. And I hated myself for that—for needing *you,* needing *us,* and needing this thing so badly.

The truth is I don't want your tenderness any more. I want your unbecoming. I want to bite the cry out of you, make your face wet with the thing you hide, and taste the salt of it while you tremble in my mouth.

But you lie so still. Beautiful. Mute. And I curl up beside you.

And that's the part I can't forgive. Not your silence. But that my body betrays me.

And I love it. And I hate it too.

The glasses were filled. *Cheers*, you said, soft, cautious, like you were testing the shape of the moment. You felt my gaze, looked up and met it. We held this between us. Your eyes were liquid, warm, soft and wet, pathetically kind, teetering on some emotional cliff. You wanted to break it—the eye contact. *Don't look at me like that*, you said, and I replied, playfully defiant, *like what?*

*Cheers*, I said, and took a sip. The space between us thinned, turned raw. Delicate. The vulnerability of it gave you away. You smiled, sad—looking for a way out, as if we were two ex-lovers, meeting over drinks, trading regrets we held for never getting our timing right, for never saying the right thing, and for never acting when we should have. Or maybe we were strangers who fucked once and couldn't shake the moment off. I smiled. Hell of a pleasant evening, that first date, first night.

We drank. We laughed. We ate. We kissed. We drank more. We laughed more. We kissed more, kissed harder, the vanilla rum slick between our teeth, lips sugary and saliva dripping. Like we were dying, and this was the last decent taste left in the world. You licked a trail down my neck, before it disappeared into my tits. I curled, sinking into your heat like a rat seeking warmth in the bin, shameless, survival-soft. It wasn't love. It was fear. It was trauma playing dress-up. *I want to sleep in this, wake in this*, I said. Maybe.

Or maybe I was already dreaming.

We'd only just met. But the hunger came in fast. Mean. Shaky. Trembling. An ache that made me say *please* without ever forming the word. Feral under the ribs, begging without language. I wanted you to press me against anything solid—wall, floor, the hard edge of your guilt—and call it love. Your hand rested on my waist, fingers splayed warm and steady. I felt your thumb graze the line of skin just above my jeans. Once. Twice. A tickle. A threat disguised as a question. I waited, heart punching bone, for you to slip the finger in. But you didn't. You just left it there. Like a tease; a fucking insult. I hated that pretty little restraint, the neutered kindness men wear when they want the cunt, but not the fallout. Do it. Do it. Do it. *Please* ...

But you didn't. Not in that moment when I needed you with animal heat, the kind that desires collision over connection. Immediate. Absolute.

And what does that make me? A slut. Maybe. Or maybe just someone who's honest. I would've fucked you right there. On the bar. On the bruise of my mother's disapproval.

At least I knew what I wanted. At least I didn't pretend. Unlike you, sipping your drink, an alibi for your cowardice. And you smiled. I hated it, I wanted to shatter it—with my mouth and with the rage of every woman who had begged without speaking, and was told—*wait*.

We were on our third drink, and I could see your guard slipping. *Three is my limit*, you said. Bullshit. It wasn't. I could tell. You didn't want to get drunk; you wanted to stay upright while watching me unravel; to be the witness, not the crime. Then came the story. A schoolyard fight. A pen. A busted nose. *I still flinch when people raise their voice*, you said. And I nodded, in that way women do when petting a man's pain. It felt like theatre: polished. You spoke like a man who'd watched a YouTube video on how to appear vulnerable. Let the words skim, just enough to glisten and pass for damage.

But I knew. It was a wound sanded down to an anecdote.

Tonight. *On my fifth drink, or maybe the sixth.* I trace you like a constellation. The boy who flinched in boarding school dorms became the man who flinched at intimacy. You built your life in compartments—neat, sterile—work, gym, friends who never asked real questions, and women who mistook stillness for depth. A people-pleaser, you were. Always did the dishes when guests stayed over, wiping counters clean—but never on Tuesdays, when it was just the two of us. You'd check in on me when I went quiet in public, whisper, *you fine?*, but never once asked what the silence meant in private. You told jokes at dinner parties, self-deprecating, charming, the kind that made people say to me, *you're lucky to have him*, and I'd smile that smile, wine-warm. You hated making people uncomfortable—except me. I was your comfort zone, your licence, and because you declared early on that you were allergic to confrontation, I became the *bitch,* aggressive by default. *Too much*. I watched you climb, slow and competent, up the professional ladder, even though it was a job you didn't love—but you did it for us, and you made sure I knew that. Your emails were polite. Your phone full of thank yous from neighbours and colleagues. You: the fella everyone called when they needed to move a couch. I knew the way you bent backwards for people who wouldn't lift a damn finger for you. I saw you nod through your boss's bullshit. Laugh off your mother's digs. Crack a smile at jokes that drew blood. I saw the exhaustion in your jaw the night you drove across the city to drop a charger for a friend who forgot hers, and came back with nothing but an apology for being late. I watched you practise adulthood like a second language—choppy, but fluent enough to pass. I saw you become a man people trusted with keys and accounts and daughters, while still, inside you, a little boy pressed against the ribs.

Still, you were funny, sometimes. The kind of funny that flickered and then went dark before anyone could warm their hands against it. You danced badly once at a wedding, and I loved you more for it. You made friends with waiters. You learnt the names of street dogs. You helped our neighbour fix her fuse, and blushed when she called you a lifesaver. I saw you, whole—the man, the boy, the actor, the ghost, the good guy who never knew what to do with goodness when it was offered back to him.

And I stayed. That's the problem with good guys. They make you want to stay. They don't give you bruises. They give you chores. They kill you in the slow leak of their absence, in all the spaces they leave empty while smiling at the world. It's the kind of emptiness you can't photograph.

How do you dump a man who hasn't done anything *wrong?* You were polite to waiters, you tipped extra, and you texted my mother on her birthday.

But you never saw me. Not really. And when I'd say that to you, you'd respond with, *what does that even mean—I don't see you? I'm here. Aren't I?* And sometimes, it made me think; maybe it's me, maybe I'm crazy, maybe I'm overthinking it. Maybe I'm *too much*.

But no.

The plants on the balcony are proof. We bought them like a fresh start, colourful pots, dirt under our nails, water can in hand—the happy life aesthetic. And for a few weeks, we were gardeners together, keepers of rituals and morning light. One day, you held the door open for a woman at the mall. A stranger. Young. Pretty. Perfumed. You'd never done it for me. Not once. And something small, stupid cracked in my chest. We didn't fight-fight. But the next morning, you didn't show up to water the plants. The can sat by the door, accusing. I waited a day, then two three. Out of spite, out of grief, out of wanting to see if you'd notice. You didn't. And by the time I gave in, touched the soil with my toe, it was already dry as bone. The leaves crisp, the stems bent. And that was how it always went with us—neglect dressed up as peace.

We didn't scream. We just stopped watering.

And in the quiet rot of our balcony, I learnt what love looked like when it died without drama; yellow leaves, soft stems, a Sunday clean-up scheduled between lunch and errands.

It was the way you gripped the back of my neck, not with lust, but like you were anchoring me in place, afraid I'd drift off into silences you couldn't fill. And I let you. Because even the wrong kind of *being held* is being held; and between now and memory, I see his face, my father's. Not the dad of childhood myths, but the one in his Raymond suit pants, unbuttoned at the waist after dinner, belly soft, watching BBC World, glasses flickering with static. The man who never raised his voice. Not even when Ma hurled the Corelle plate that smashed just short of his feet. He blinked, picked up the pieces, mumbled, *it's alright it's alright*, like peace was a fucking spell he could whisper into the shards.

You groaned, and I kissed you. Open. Messy. A punch. As if I could suck that man out of my bloodstream. I bit down. You twitched. Not in pleasure, but in polite confusion. I clawed at your chest, not to arouse, but to leave proof. That I was here. That I existed.

And he turned his face towards me, with that helpless look. Like life had happened to him. I hated that look. It made me want to smash glass. Grab his collar and scream: DO something. DEFEND me. Pick a side. Pick mine. But he never did.

So I bit my tongue until I tasted blood—a reminder that I was alive; anything to erase him. Then you kissed my wrist. Held it there, in your palm, delicate and holy, said, *you smell like burnt sugar*; and for one dumb godless second, everything stilled, and I believed you. My body fluttered, sick, clenched, stupid with hope. And I thought, *maybe. Just maybe. There's still a way out.*

Sometimes it hits me later—a quiet shame nesting under the ribs like a squealing rat.

From the early days: I can picture the flick of my thumb on your lighter, the laughter that came out too high, too damn eager when you said my name like it was yours to say. The way I glanced at the mirror behind you just to catch your eyes still on me, as if your gaze could staple me to the room, keep me from drifting like a useless receipt. I leaned in. I always lean in. And I let your eyes crawl over me. Let your silence pass for mystery, even when it is just a lack of courage. I brushed your knee with mine, begged without begging, and gave you the kind of smile my mother would have slapped off my face.

You were kind. New. Fresh-scrubbed with potential.

And I?

I was already moving furniture in my head, picturing your toothbrush next to mine, your socks in my drawer. First date. First date. First. Fucking. Date. I screamed in my head, and still, I asked, out of the blue, drunk, absent-minded, *what's your type*? Soft bristles, you said, and I filed it away like it meant something. Like the universe had handed me a sign that you might stay. That this time, I might be kept.

And in the quiet between jokes, sips and lazy kissing, I felt it—the mangy little animal in my chest, pacing, gnawing at the bars, hissing, not to be alone again not to be alone again not to be alone again. I felt it in my jaw, that wild pulse, a rattle up my spine, like I might sob or bite or drop to my knees right there on the bar floor, sticky chip-chip, under the flickering lights, begging you to keep the last warm thing in me from going cold.

But I didn't. I just grinned. Bit down on my straw, said something cute about the fucking weather, how the air was thick, like it knew something it wouldn't say. Meanwhile, I was choking on everything I couldn't ask. Protect me, I wanted to say, *from the mornings* that arrive teeth-first, with calendars and news alerts and emails about nothing. From the way people speak like answers exist. From the sun—burning pervert, bastard spotlight—that makes me feel real again. But I swallowed it. Because women like me don't beg. Not out loud. And I hoped to god you'd see through me. Past the lip gloss and the practised nods. Past the part of me that wants to ruin and run. See the feral silence between my teeth, and stay.

We tipped the last of our drinks into plastic cups and stepped out. Closing time. And you, ever the functional little man, flagged a rick. Let's walk, I said, craving more night, more wrong, more maybe. You turned sheepish—that surrendered tilt of your head I'd come to know too well—and you apologized to the rick guy. A silent flare went through me. *A little coward you are*, I thought, *the kind who never risks offending anyone but me*, and *sorry*, you repeated, *sorry bhaiyya, sorry*. The apology patient, so fucking polite, it felt obscene; and it made me want to kiss you, or kill you. Maybe both. Probably both.

But that was sweet of you. Pathetic, but sweet.

And we walked. Two fools merry on a footpath not meant for romance. The streetlamps hung, draped in orange fog. They watched us pass with their dying yellow dots, whispering, *look at them look at them look at them*. The heat of the day clung, sticky and unshaken. Your hand brushed mine. Once. Twice. Not a grip. Just a maybe. And I didn't pull away. I didn't lean in either. We just let our arms dangle beside each other, like children too shy to speak.

And we kept walking. No direction. Just the rhythm of our soles slapping against dust and piss. Shops shuttered. Dogs barking. A scooter grazing past, clipping the air; I flinched. You said nothing. Just kept walking. That's what you always did. Witnessed the near-collisions and let them be. We passed a paan shop. You stopped to light a cigarette, hands trembling. You cupped the flame, and I watched your face glow. I wanted to say, *you're beautiful like this*. I wanted to say, *please don't be kind to me tonight. I don't need it.* Instead, I asked for a drag. You passed it over, quiet. Our fingers touched. Static. It zapped something in my chest. I took the pull. It hit sharp. Burnt good. We walked past a sad-ass pole, flyers bleeding ink, big REWARD letters shouting about some lost cat no one was gonna find, and a tea stall, closed but scented from the day's rush. The air reeked of milk and cardamom. For a second, just one soft second, I wanted to sit on the still-warm ledge, take off my shoes, and tell you everything. But I didn't. *Careful*, you said, and we stepped over a wet patch that screamed vomit and last chances. I said something dumb. You laughed. Not because it was funny, but because it was time to laugh. Then, you reached for my hand, your fingers found mine. No ask. No ceremony. Just there. Casual. Almost accidental. And I didn't pull away. I let it happen. Swinging between sin and something softer. The contact lingered longer than it should have. Longer than new people are supposed to allow. Our palms went slick, then stupidly wet. Clammy. Embarrassed. And still, you didn't let go. Not even when I twitched my wrist. Not even when I trembled. You held on, like a fucking leash. And I let you. Not because I couldn't free myself, but because for one more street, one more breath, I wanted to feel owned. And already, I dreaded the moment when you'd let go; and my hand, this hand, the same one *holding a drink tonight, fifth or sixth,* I don't know I don't know I don't know, wet still, would feel the loss like a severed limb. Because when you let go, I'd have no one to blame but myself. And what's worse than loneliness? Knowing you welcomed it in. Let it fuck you raw, and made it breakfast the next morning.

I looked at you then. Really looked. The tight line of your jaw. The exhausted corners of your mouth. The way your beauty was half apology. And the sadness stitched into your posture. I thought: *Maybe … I can fix this*. And I hated myself for it. Because I've tried this before. Because I know how the movie ends. And still, we kept walking. Not towards a home. Just away from the ending.

Because once it ends, we'll have to decide. Whether to kiss. Or leave. Or pretend none of this ever meant a thing.

There were mornings you'd wake before me, clanging around the kitchen like a man who meant well. You'd bring me coffee just how I like it—no sugar, one teaspoon of milk (you always overboiled it, bless you), and whisper, *rise up, my terror*. There were nights you'd fall asleep mid-sentence, but your arm would still reach for me in the dark. Not love. Just reflex. Muscle memory. As if some old part of you knew I'd drift, leave silently. And you remembered things. The brand of soap from my mother's bathroom, Liril, that neon-green sin of nostalgia, bastard of a scent. You remembered, even though I said it just once, and in a fight. I hated you for it—for a tenderness that doesn't know how to save, but still shows up. That day, when I bled through my skirt in that overpriced bar at Khan Market, crimson blooming, shame on linen, you didn't flinch. Just took off your jacket and tied it around me. Not chivalry. Not pity. Just a wordless acknowledgement that bodies leak. You always offered your hand first, even after fights. Even when I didn't deserve it. Even when you were aware that I could bite. Really bite.

These little things. Fuck. They got in. Stitched something in me. And that was enough to make me stay. And I hated it. Hated that the tiniest gestures—your half-burnt toast offerings, your stupid clumsy kisses that landed on my eyebrow instead of my cheek—could unmake me more thoroughly than all the polished silences. Hated that I waited for them. Craved them like junkie shit—the hit, tender; the comedown, violent. Hated that I forgave you. That I'd trade a week of cold shoulders for a single moment of you refilling my glass without asking. Hated that I loved the man you were when you were trying, even if it only lasted three minutes, and smelt of toothpaste and sleep.

Someplace inside this snarling wreck, I want to believe there's breath left. A lung holding on. Enough to keep my cunt warm at the memory of your hand on my thigh at traffic lights. Enough to remember that once, you tucked my hair behind my ear and didn't say anything clever. Didn't joke. Didn't ruin it. Just *did it*. And the silence that followed? It didn't sting. It rested. Sat beside me like an old dog. Heavy. Familiar. Just enough.

In those early times, hope didn't even feel like hope. It felt like fact—inevitable, dumb and certain.

Like that Sunday morning you made us eggs—burnt at the edges, yolk burst, salt forgotten—but you placed them on a chipped plate and said, *for my favourite bitch*. And I laughed. Not because it was funny, but because you were mine. And you were here.

Or the time I came back from that shit meeting, and you just pulled me to your chest, didn't ask, didn't talk, just *held*. Let me cry into the smell of your underarm and Axe body spray.

Or that cheap-ass date night at Select City where we couldn't afford a meal, so we bought popcorn and one large Pepsi with two straws, and you kept nudging the tub towards me, saying, *you take the caramel ones*. I knew you liked them more. And I pretended not to melt. But my fingers shook when I reached in, sticky with sugar and hunger, and I hated that you could make me soft with so little. I think you noticed; and I wanted you to notice. I wanted to be chosen in these small, stupid ways. That was the first time it hit, like a dirty epiphany: *Fuck, this is it.*

You used to write me notes. Not poems. But grocery lists where you'd sneak in: condoms + banana + call your mom + I love your face today. That kind of stupid. You'd wake up before me, always, and brush your teeth in the dark so the light wouldn't hit my eyes. Sometimes, you'd trip over your sneakers, and curse under your breath, and I'd bite my pillow to swallow the laugh, and the love, and the ache of knowing I'd already built a shrine out of your clumsiness. That Diwali, we didn't do anything, not even light a lamp, but you held my hand under the blanket, while the crackers shook the glass, and said, *we don't need light, we got this.*

And the fights. We had those too. But you always came back. Even if it was just to sit beside me on the floor, drinking from my glass, not yours. Saying mine tasted better. I don't think you knew that made me cry. Not from sadness, but from how seen I felt.

I kept a running list. Of every time you showed up when I didn't think you would. Every time you didn't flinch. Every time your voice cracked and you didn't try to hide it. I inked that shit into my bones. Made myths out of mornings. Gospel out of leftovers. Because in the beginning, you weren't perfect, but you were trying. And I would've built an afterlife out of your trying.

One night, back in those early half-sweet months, August maybe, or September: the light was forgiving, the fan too loud, and you said something offhand, lazy-cruel in that casual way you had. It landed sharp, and I went quiet. You panicked. I could feel it, that tiny crack in your voice, the pathetic tremble as you scrambled to cover it. *Let's have a baby*, you said. Like it was a joke. Or a dare. Or an apology wearing a clown mask. And I said, *okay*. Flat. No wink. No bluff. Just the word. Your eyes flicked. I saw it. That little fracture in your calm. You weren't built for follow-through. You were the maestro of almost. The conductor of maybe. But this? This was real. So, you kissed me: defiant, too fast, too clumsy. Climbed on top, fumbling with your belt like it meant something. And I let you. I let it all happen while watching your face. I thought—*ah, there you are, the man-boy, the crack behind the swagger*.

You didn't mean it. You thought I'd laugh, say no, call your bluff. But I didn't. And, now, you were scrambling for the emergency exit with your dick out. And you found your way out. Eventually. But I'd seen *it*. The flash of fear. It sat between us like that child we never made. Quiet. Breathing. Knowing.

It began with bullshit things. Always does. You still made coffee, but stopped asking how I slept. You still touched my back in bed, but it felt like habit, not heat. You still texted when you were late, but the messages got shorter. No emojis. No kiss at the end. Just logistics. You started saying *we'll see* more than *yeah sure*. You stopped laughing at my bad jokes. You'd sit beside me on the sofa, but with your knees facing the other way. You didn't notice when

I stopped wearing perfume. And dinners went quiet. Not angry. Just ... like the food mattered more than us. You praised the daal. *Tastes good*, you said. Not: *You make it better each time*. You didn't mean harm. But the weight of that missing sentence jabbed. And slowly, my questions changed too. From *are you okay* to *did you take the milk out?* From *where do you hurt* to *can you pass the salt?*

Our bodies still touched. We fucked, still. Less hunger, more tradition. Like folding laundry: necessary, joyless. I stopped moaning. Not in protest. It just didn't come. You didn't notice. And when you turned off the light, you didn't check if I was facing you. I wasn't.

You were still kind. Still decent. Still there. But I was already mourning.

So, I tried fixing it. Like a dumbass. With overcompensation. With effort. The kind that stinks of desperation. Started folding your T-shirts the way your mother did—shoulder to shoulder, tight and neat, as if order could hold us together, bribe love back into the room. I cooked elaborate meals on weekdays, risottos, lamb chops, fancy shit, meals we'd eat silently, chewing like the food might say what we couldn't. I laughed louder at your work stories. Nodded. Waxed. Bleached. Shaved it, turning my body into a lie, polite for your gaze. I wore the blue dress you once said looked good, even though it clung in the wrong places. I memorized your colleague's names. Started texting you *good luck* for meetings. I made playlists. Love songs. Subtle ones. Hidden like prayers. I smiled more. Bit my tongue more. Made more space for your quiet. Pretended your distance was just exhaustion, work, traffic. I planned Sunday picnics in parks you strolled past. Booked date nights you postponed. Lit candles you didn't notice. Wore lingerie that scratched and bit, just to feel wanted, and to make want possible again. And I moaned. Loud. Too loud. Performance-level. Oscar-worthy. Sometimes. You kissed me after. Told me I felt good. But not once did you look me in the eyes. And every time you rolled away, I thought maybe it was me. Maybe I needed to be gentler. Thinner. Calmer. Less. And still ...

It was like drowning in a toilet that's seen too much action—shit piss puke. That's how it felt. That first night. Then. Now. Ache masquerading as a moment. Overdressed and underfed. Trying to play it cool while the insides clawed with longing stretched too thin. The night pressed, velvet with an absence, humming hollow behind the ribs. It leaked out of me. And then, you said something about the sky. How the stars looked fake. How Delhi air never deserved this much beauty. I nodded like I gave a shit. Like I wasn't already watching your mouth, wondering how long till it would be on mine. And I wanted to cry—snot fists and childhood. The sort that makes a man reconsider touching a woman again.

But I didn't cry. It's something I'd been working on, like how to not hate myself at 3 a.m.

We are walking, still, but it's beginning to get stupid. You lead gently, like you think I'll break. And maybe I will. But not the way you think. Not fragile like glass, but like a grenade.

We reach a spot, dark, hidden somewhat, a hideout between two buildings. And you turn, slow, like a priest about to sin, and ask, *can I kiss you?* It's permission you seek. *So sweet*, I think, and it disarms me, your voice quivering like winter, as if it's your first time asking for anything. I almost laugh. Not cruelly. Not at you. But at the absurdity of it. That even here, even now, with the night practically humping our legs, you seek permission.

How refreshing. How fucking rare.

I look at you—really look. You have that schoolboy's guilt look, like a guy who'll say *please* while he's deep inside me. It should turn me off. It doesn't. I'm a sucker for good manners.

There is music in the distance. A remix of something old … something with ache baked in. And beneath me, an itch. Because I've already said yes.

I said it when I touched your knee back at the bar. Said it when, slurred with drink, you licked a trail down my neck, and I whispered, *I want to sleep in this, wake in this*. Said it when I imagined your hand at my throat—not tight, just enough to say, *you're here, you're mine, shut the fuck up*. That a *yes* had already bloomed under the table, begging to be pressed.

And now your voice comes, unsure; and I crumble. A small internal collapse. It doesn't show on my face. But inside, the bitch barks hungry feral hopeful *fuck me fuck me fuck me—shut up shut up shut up*. I bite on the leash, the thoughts yanking my gut. Your hand brushes against my waist, and my body short-circuits. Not the romantic kind of shiver. No. It's lower. Darker. Like a warning light, red, spinning under my belly button, triggering nerve endings like exposed wires. The edge of your fingers rests at the band of my jeans, and I want to scream. *Go lower, you idiot. Just go. Don't make me guide you. Do it. Do it. Do it. Please …*

But you don't. You stop. Like a good man. And I hate good men, I think. I hate that they always stop, make you wait, and I nod. I smile. And soaked with begging, *yes please*, I whisper. Yes, I say aloud, clutching at the possibility that maybe this one won't end with me cleaning myself off in your bathroom at 2 a.m. And you smile, soft like a church candle. Like someone handed you fire and said, *be careful now*. And it ruins me a little, your smile; it makes me want to believe in kindness again. Your hands hesitate, stupid with courtesy, trembling butterflies on roadkill. You hover. Maybe you can smell it on me, that wet-dog stink of desperation. You linger there, and I should laugh. Should tell you to go home. But I don't. I wait. Like always. Like I'd been trained to. And then you move in, lips nervous, afraid of messing it up, and I meet you there, in that space between what we want and what we settle for. A pause. Your lips brush mine. And everything breaks. Contact. Finally. Not soft. Not savage. Just enough.

You kiss me like you are grateful. And fuck me, I know that look. That soft pause, the please in your lips. Like a man who's never been wanted without conditions attached. I have no time for your learning curve. So I go in, teeth-first, and kiss you dirty saliva wild. Because fuck poetry. Fuck timing. This isn't romance. This is collateral damage. *Help me* disguised as *take me*. Your lips taste like guilt. And I swallow it. My body lunges, too eager, a traitor in the shape of a woman. No spine. All mouth. A dumb bitch in heat. Open in ways I don't consent to. And when your tongue meets mine, I flinch. It's instinct. History. A girl learns how to brace. I don't moan. I bite. Hard. You pause. Good. I want you to wear it. The wound. The receipt. I want your friends to notice the purple smudge on your lip, and for you to lie; to say, *it was a fight, a stumble, a wild night*. Not me. Never say my name. I am nothing to brag about.

Halfway through it, the kiss turns. Starts off all hot mouths and drunk heat, but then, it shifts. It isn't a kiss any more. It's an ambush. A room with no exit. One minute we're just swapping spit, the next, hell breaks loose in slow motion. Brick by brick. Breath by breath. A goddamn building collapse of bad decisions. This is not foreplay. It's a murder-suicide pact between our tongues. You kiss like you're trying to eat your way through every year I wasn't wanted. I respond like I'm trying to choke down every year I was. There's blood in it, and the taste of Old Monk—vanilla-metallic. And I taste, too, childhood and death, and rust and shame. I taste my own name chewed up and spat back at me by boys who said they cared. I taste every time I said yes when I wanted to scream. But I don't pull away. I go deeper. Harder. Hoping to find the girl who stopped asking to be touched gently. My thoughts blur. The world shrinks. There is only the burn of your fingers at the edge of my jeans, the friction of thigh on thigh, and the press of your need against mine like we owe each other something. And then, your hands. They stop quivering. One slides up under my shirt. I gasp like I've been stabbed. Not because it hurts, but because it doesn't. Because it feels close to *right;* and I am not ready for that—the softness dressed as want; and my body, stupid-traitor-slut, melts like it hasn't been touched in years: bone softened by time, slow deep, and without flair. And my hands, they are in your hair, fisting—rummaging through your adolescence, not out of tenderness, but to make sure you stay. Stay buried in me. Stay stupid. Stay mine. And somewhere between tongue and pant, I realize I'm not kissing you any more. I'm kissing absence. I'm kissing every boy who said, *you're not like other girls*, as if it were a compliment. I'm kissing every man who told me I was too much too loud too complicated. I'm kissing history. Kissing the fucking void. And the void, baby, it's kissing me back.

We grind, pressed against the side of a taxi like animals trying to out-hurt the past. You take my drink, still locked in and set it on the roof of the taxi, never breaking from me. We devour. We desecrate. It's not love. It's penance. My breath stutters, hiccups caught between a sob and a laugh. We're both trying to get beneath each other's ribs, fumbling for soul, but settling for skin. It's not foreplay. It's *foredamage*. So, we cling, pretending touch is therapy. We aren't fucking. We are testifying. I moan. A death rattle, ash in lungs. You suck it in. And then: We break for air, and my head spins. I see stars behind your eyes. Or maybe it's vodka blindness, or the sheer fucking fact that your mouth still tastes like sin, and I'm starving. You grunt like a boy mid-wet-dream, your breath crashing into my face, rough and salt-tanged. My legs are wax. And still I want more. Always more. I kiss the sweat off your neck, holy and mine. Your thumb brushes my jaw. *Again*, you mutter. I let out a breathless laugh, and look at you. Really look. Stupid face. Beautiful wreck. Yeah. Again. But harder this time.

And here we are, again. Your eyes, red-rimmed, bleary, some mix of rum and guilt. And mine? Worse. Twitchy and teetering, that bastard muscle under my eye doing its thing, a warning shot. The kind of twitch that says: *Get out, sweetheart*. Says: *This man won't rescue you, but he might be good enough to hold your hair back while you puke at 3 a.m*. And I look into you—cracked red and heavy, drunk, exhausted—for any signs of fairytale endings, *the happily ever after*. A love found. A love Neptune, so far so unattainable, and so blue, it bruises. A love 4.6195 billion kilometres away. Cold. Icy. Pointless. We do not part. We should've. My fault. Should've walked out the minute I saw that sad little apology living behind your smile—the kind that doesn't mean anything. The kind that's just a reflex. You said *sorry* to the rickshaw guy when I said *let's walk*, and that did it. That's when I knew. You're too soft to love a woman like me. Fucking pussy. And I hate how wet that makes me. So I want to leave. I must. My body's screaming for it—*leave leave leave*—the way it screamed when I was thirteen and some uncle put his hand on my knee, and called me mature. My knee remembers. But my feet? They stayed. Nailed by hope. By inertia. By some fucking internal illness called maybe-this-time.

And tonight, at Bar-Bar, that song soft through the speakers is floaty familiarity, an ache like perfume—*leave leave leave.* NOW. *Enough tonight; the drinks, fifth or sixth.* I don't know. Let's go, I say. But we don't. We can't. Because home; it's a fucking war zone. Carpeted in eggshells. Wallpapered in, just kidding. Love there means breaking first, hugging second.

And now, in remembrance, I linger.

Why didn't you walk away that night? Why didn't I? We should have. But that's the thing about damage. It doesn't need a grand entrance. Doesn't knock. It just drifts in, barefoot and quiet. Makes itself comfortable. Like dust. Like shame. Like a love that never lit the sky, but simply flickered in the corner, waiting to die. Not sacred. Just … inevitable.

We didn't fucking leave. Even when the night soured, turned mean vinegar in the veins; we stayed we stayed we stayed. My spine whispered it first, that low ancient ache at the base; get—out—now. But I didn't. Couldn't. Not because I was in love. No. I was stitched to you by something uglier; a leash disguised as chemistry; a hunger I didn't want to admit to, because admitting it would mean confessing how starved I'd been. You held nothing for me. Nothing *real;* except some busted chord of shared damage and history. My skin said stay. My gut said run. And my heart, just curled up, too tired to pick a side.

So we stayed. Because that's what we do. We don't leave. We *linger.* Not out of hope, but out of pattern.

And maybe that's the truth of it. Maybe that's what we were from the start. A warning label, a cautionary tale with nowhere to go.

And now that goddamn song, you know the one, *our* song, plays again. Low, slippery, bleeding from the speakers at Bar-Bar. Muffled and cheap. The night mocking me with a playlist. It terrifies me, that melody. Not because it reminds me of love, but because it reminds me of delusion. Of hope we didn't deserve. I want to throw the glass at the wall at your face at mine. But I don't. I just sip. Smile. Swallow the scream like a good girl. *On my fifth drink, or maybe the sixth.* I don't know I don't know I don't know. And maybe that's the point. Maybe this isn't even a feeling any more. Maybe it's a mood, heavy in the bones. A parasite, humming electric under the skin. And it stays. Long after the sugar's gone from the drinks, and the bar stools are flipped. It stays like a child we didn't plan, didn't name; and still, we rock it, feed it, cradle it, sing to it bittersweet lullabies of *what-ifs*.

We should've flushed the mood out. But we didn't. We made room for it between us. And now the past isn't the past any more. Not tonight. It's sticky. It drips. That night, *this* night, keeps playing behind my eyes like an old tape, the kind that makes you think it was tender, because it's grainy. It wasn't tender. It was a con-job in candlelight. And we rewind it again and again, not to reminisce, but to interrogate, to look for the exact frame when we broke. The pixel where we fell out of rhythm. When we said or did the wrong thing. Laid eyes on each other in a way that was too much or not enough. A gesture misfired. A laugh that cut too sharp. A silence mistaken for cruelty. And then came the apologies, endless—fucking—apologies, offered not to each other, but to the scene. To the idea of us. To the imaginary couple with better lighting and better lines. And we weren't apologizing for the pain. We were saying sorry for breaking out of character. For ruining the fantasy. For forgetting our marks and fucking up the timing. We rehearsed it in our heads. The clever quips, the tears at the right beat, the long looks like goddamn movie stills. And every time we missed the cue; every time I said the honest thing too early or you shut down too soon, we'd start over, re-shoot the scene. Night after night. New drinks. New dialogue. Same old tragedy.

Let's try again. Maybe this time.

*I'm sorry.*

*Me too.*

Not for what we did, but for what we failed to become. As if the love would have worked if only we'd delivered our lines better. As if we were one good edit away from the fairy tale. Repeat. *Sorry. Please. Sorry. Please. Sorry. Please.*

And that's the cruellest part. It's not memory any more. It's residue. Fog. A phantom ache. And we don't know, still, exactly how we fucked it, but we know we did.

So, we stay. Not because there's something left to save, but because there's nowhere else to go.

We do the dishes like inmates on kitchen duty. Backs bent, mouths shut, wrists moving in rhythm, to a sentence neither of us can remember pleading guilty to. The clink of plates, the soft slap of suds—a language older than love. You hand me the tea towel as if it is a peace treaty you don't believe in. I dry the knife like it might remember the argument we didn't have. We talk of potholes, petrol rates, and the lack of trees. I nod. Give you a *hmm.*

It's the first time, but it lands, that soft slippery murmur of surrender. *Hmm.* It says I heard you, and I can't fight this. Don't ask what's wrong. Don't poke the bruise. I don't know where to begin. You blink. Then nod. *Hmm,* you reply. And there it is. The beginning of the end. We don't go quiet all at once. We drip into silence. Not with drama. Just with … *hmms.* They become scaffolding. *Hmm,* when I ask if you're hungry. *Hmm,* when I cry in the bathroom and pretend I'm brushing. *Hmm,* when we fuck, and you finish too fast. *Hmm,* when I say I'm tired, and you say, *me too*. It becomes code. Safety. A straitjacket that feels like skin. We build a home in it. Furnish it with soggy kisses and sighs. *Hmm* is the wallpaper. *Hmm* is the bed. And on nights when you reach for my thigh, I turn into you with a small polite *hmm.* Not a yes. Not a no. Just consent shaped silence. The kind that doesn't stop anything. Doesn't start anything either. You breathe heavier, maybe relieved, maybe not, and I close my eyes. We fuck like mountains. And when it ends; because it always ends, you roll away, and I roll in, and between *us* is a space just wide enough to fit every version of what we were, and what we could have been.

A decade *Hmm*-ed, version 1. You say—I say.

You say: Should we switch to oat milk again?
I say: *Hmm (tired).*

You say: Almond takes too much water to produce.
I say: *Hmm (bored).*

You say: Traffic's hell.
I say: *Hmm (scrolling).*

You say: The AC's making me sick.
I say: *Hmm (uninterested).*

You say: My boss wants a deck by 9 a.m.
I say: *Hmm (just fog).*

You say: Your towel's on my hook again.
I say: *Hmm (unmoved).*

You say: We're out of toilet paper.
I say: *Hmm (fix it).*

You say: Cook or order in?
I say: *Hmm (don't care).*

You say: Your mom called.
I say: *Hmm (don't ask me to call back).*

You say: You left the geyser on again.
I say: *Hmm (so what).*

You say: Can we talk about this weekend?
I say: *Hmm (rather not).*

You say: You've been quiet lately.
I say: *Hmm (you noticed).*

You say: I didn't mean it like that.
I say: *Hmm (then why say it).*

You say: Do you still want this?
I say: *Hmm (define—this).*

You say: Should we try therapy?
I say: *Hmm (whatever).*

You say: Let's not fight.
I say: *Hmm (too fucking late).*

You say: I miss *us.*
I say: *Hmm (sad, angry).*

You say: I love you.
I say: *Hmm (you sure?).*

You say: Did you hear me?
I say: *Hmm (I did).*

You say: What are we doing?
I say: *Hmm (closest I get to a scream).*

A decade *Hmm*-ed, version 2. I say—You say.

I say: Remember the last time we fucked?
You say: *Hmm (dodging).*

I say: I changed my shampoo to the one you liked.
You say: *Hmm (scrolling).*

I say: You don't ask about my day any more.
You say: *Hmm (vague guilt, instantly swallowed).*

I say: My mother called. Asked if I'm happy.
You say: *Hmm (sidestepping).*

I say: I saw a photo of us from three years ago.
You say: *Hmm (resigned).*

I say: There is a spider in the bathroom.
You say: *Hmm (so* now *you need me).*

I say: I've been thinking of quitting my job.
You say: *Hmm (don't).*

I say: You take me for granted.
You say: *Hmm (I know).*

I say: Let's not talk in code any more.
You say: *Hmm (still code).*

I say: You remember when we …
You say: *Hmm (already done).*

I say: Fuck me like before.
You say: *Hmm (confused).*

I say: We need to talk.
You say: *Hmm (no, or worse, yes).*

I say: I loved you, you know.
You say: *Hmm (me too).*

I say: Say something. Anything. Break this.
You say: *Hmm (let's not).*

And now, we fuck on Saturdays; because that's the day we fuck. The day the sheets are changed, the fridge cleaned, and the bins taken out. You enter like you're clocking in. No foreplay. Just function. Dick. Duty. Done. Your breath reeks of toothpaste and indifference; and the thrusts, even, polite like footsteps in a hallway. I lift my legs, good girl, goddamn favour, a courtesy, and you finish quick. We don't make love any more we make evidence. That we're still here. Still trying. And that should count for something? A love that went too far—and not far enough. You mutter goodnight. I give you a *Hmm.* A nod that says thank you for the fuck, sir. You're welcome. And then I lie in the dark, a dead, gutted thing, breathing, still, out of spite. But there's something grotesquely honest in it. A need buried so deep in the rot it smells medicinal. Like pus. Proof that the body is still flinching at the wound. I worship it. The yellow milky grace. A fantasy dripping in guilt, filthy-scabbed. Good for masturbating.

We used to touch with hunger. Now, we inventory our love between mouthfuls of hmms and silence. *Ssh* … listen carefully. There's some pulse left in it. More twitch than beat. A muscle memory of wanting that fires in the absence of hope. Locked in the bathroom, mouth stuffed with undies, I use it. Use *you*. The memory of us in better lighting. Of your hands, once trembling on my thighs. Of your voice, seeking permission. The light flickers, gasps. It knows what's about to happen. Wants no part of it. The floor is cold, tiles cracked. I sit on it anyway, spine against the wall, knees spread like a confession, and I touch myself to the echo of your apologies. Hard. Not sweet. Not tender. Three fingers deep. Fast. Ugly. Friction ache and urgency. Like scratching an itch that won't quit. And I don't do it for pleasure. I do it for proof. That your weight on me was real, and the decade of happily ever after had some happy in it. That I mattered. That your weight once pinned me

to something real. That I was touched. My elbow knocks into the bucket. Water laps against plastic, sloshes out, pooling puddles under my ass. I don't stop. I don't moan. I chew down on the cotton, grunt like an animal giving birth. And I come with a grunt, *fuccccck* I scream, choked off into the undies. Not from joy, but from the cruelty of remembering, wanting what no longer exists.

And the underwear slips out of my mouth, slick with spit, thick with something worse than spit. Shame? Maybe. Or just another fluid in a night full of bad decisions. Then, I wipe myself with your towel, and hang it back on the hook. And now it feels as if we were never anything, not lovers, not married, not even decent mistakes. Just two tired fucks playing house in a set that looked like love from far away. No final bow. No applause. Just blackout.

And I?

I'd still take it, I think. Even now. Even like this.

*Fifth drink. Sixth. Seventh.* I don't know. The bartender pours and I nod, a god accepting worship. You're not here, but your voice is, gnawing through what's left of my restraint. The glass sweats. And here we are, again. Ten years of groceries and gas bills. Of scraping burnt toast into the sink. Of *what time are you coming home* and *did you eat*? Of dirty dishes passed like indictments. Of cold tea, untouched. Of watching the rice boil over. Of warm beer. Of the sour smell of old laundry breath and fights. Of waiting in bathrooms, scrolling scrolling pretending. Of finishing the Netflix show you started, because screw it, why wait for him. Of fucks given, and fucks postponed. Of walking back into rooms we'd stormed out of, too tired to stay mad, too bitter to say sorry. And when it got too ugly, there's the bell. A little brass fucker we bought off a street vendor in Varanasi.

We made rules. Ding the bell, fight's done. No matter how deep the cut. How loud the slam. Reset. Ha.

You rang it like a goddamn rimshot. Punchline to pain. Right after you said, *you always do this*, and just before I could spit *fuck you*, then—ding ding ding—closing the tab. Cue the silence. And I followed. Caught on. Learnt how to use it like a cheat code. Ring it before he gets the last word in. Ring it before I lose control. Ring it to win. Ring it to shut him down. We rang it mid-tears mid-slap mid-truth and mid-me, finally saying what I should've said. And yes, for a hot minute, it worked. Because we were stupid enough to believe it would.

And now?

Now it's a joke. The bell rings hollow. Flat. Dead. We ring it out of habit. Out of spite. Trying to resuscitate each other by slapping the air. A farce—ding ding ding—that sound echoes through this mausoleum of happily ever after. And still, we stay. Because leaving takes guts. And staying: just inertia. I take a sip. I get back home, I think, *but I don't.* Because I know what'll follow. Slap. Slap. Repeat. Ten years of that too. I kick my shoes off. You don't look up. I say something cruel. You lob back with a *hmm.* I should've left when I had the chance. Bitch, you say that every week; and here you are. Yeah. Like mould. We laugh.

Then—out of nowhere—I slap myself; full palm cracked, like bitter punctuation. You blink. *We decided we aren't doing that any more*, you say. I do it again. Red bloom rising. You scream, hit yourself too, eyes gleaming with spite, or pride. I can't tell. *This is what you want, don't you?* I grin. And now, it's a tennis match. Left cheek. Right. We go back and forth, trading hits. Then, I veer. Find your face. You don't flinch. Your lips part, and I see it, primal-raw. I know what's next. Your hand lifts. Connects. Crack. I return the favour. And we go at it again, a metronome of madness. You slap me. I slap you. Enough to bruise, to say, *I'm still here I'm still here I'm still here. Still flesh. Still fire.* And when we're spent, skin stinging, hearts ragged, we stand inches apart. Too close. Breathing each other's ghosts.

I want to kiss you. You want to kill me. Neither of us moves.

You vanish into the bathroom. I sit there, cheeks hot, cigarette trembling between two fingers. The fan above spins, still, an executioner too slow to be merciful, and I wonder, fuck, have we always been like this? Did we crawl into this hell with open eyes, or was it stitched into that first kiss? Some cursed choreography we mistook for chemistry? You flush. I light another, and exhale into the hush between us. Soon, it'll be winter again; and our soft breaths, foggy, will announce a truce. Your hand will find my thigh, and I'll open, because I believe. One blink and we're here; another, and I'm back to that first night. There was laughter. A drink too many. Something shared. The way a wrist was touched. I remember thinking, *this will be the start of something beautiful or the undoing of everything*. Maybe it rained that night. Or maybe I imagined the rain later, like a detail added in a story told too often.

You return. Sit beside me. Your knee against mine. My heart doesn't jump, but it does shift. Like an old dog rising in its sleep. Your head leans till it touches mine, barely. And for a second, we're not bitter. Not bruised. Not broken. Just tired animals in the dark, leaning in for warmth. I don't speak. I don't have to. I just think: *Let this be enough*. And maybe, you're thinking it too.

It was me. I slapped first—an out-of-nowhere kind of whack, a flat-palmed fuck you, sudden and regretful. I don't remember when, or for what, but I remember clearly. It was me. Year two, or three. And I remember, too, your reaction. I was hoping for you to hit me back, but you didn't. You just left the room, wanting to be alone with the hit. That calm—it wasn't mercy. It was the way you won without saying a word. It was victory. You just sat there on the edge of the couch, legs spread enough to take up space, one hand resting on your knee, the other cradling your glass like it might spill if you so much as twitched. You didn't drink from it. You let the ice melt. Your head tilted, eyes level, breathing so steady it made me feel rabid by comparison. Pulse in my teeth, sweaty lips, knees bouncing, trying to shake the fight out of me. I was the storm. You were the eye.

And without moving, or saying a damn word, you made me feel like the crazy one. The loud one. The bitch. And you knew it. You were counting the seconds. Sitting higher every time I twitched. It made my skin crawl, that power you had in doing nothing. The way you could make me feel small without a single insult. And the more you sat there, still and smug, with your drink and monk pose, the more I boiled. Till the heat under my ribs turned to stone. I wanted to see it crack. I wanted to see you crack. A slip. A goddamn blink. Something to prove you were still human.

But you didn't. And that's how you won.

So next time, I make it deliberate. Like art. Not a flailing slap of regret. No. This one's born with teeth. It's the morning after a fight, and we are still on edge. I wait. I watch. Let your nerves fray just enough. Let your temper simmer like a pot forgotten on the stove. I feed it with little things—deliberate sabotage, a question asked twice, eyes rolled, a yawn, and a slow sip while you're talking, like your words don't mean shit. And I can see it rising, the twitch in your jaw, the way you roll your shoulders like the air's too tight. And then, I step close. So close I can smell the stale bite of last night's rum on your breath. I tilt my head, smile just enough to be insulting. And I slap you. Hard. Not a warning tap. Not a lover's tease. I put my whole goddamn arm into it, shoulder to palm, rage to bone. The crack of it fills the room. Hot bloom across my fingers. Your face whips sideways like a page turned too fast. And I wait for the return fire. The gut punch. The shove. The fuck-you-bitch. But you don't give me that. You look at me, eyes black with something I can't name, and then, you slap yourself. Once. Twice. A third time, faster, louder, the sound obscene in the narrow room. Your palm snaps against your skin in a rhythm too quick to be rage. It's something filthier. Quieter. A punishment dressed up as performance. By the fifth, your cheek is bright and raw, your breath coming short, your mouth curling into something between a grin and a grimace. Is that it? You spit and hit yourself again.

And I?

I just watch. My hand still tingling from the first slap, my pulse low and steady. Because you're showing off, saying, *look what I can do to me; you're nothing*. And that's the worst part, you telling me you can hurt yourself better than I ever can. And I fucking hate you for it. And I hate how much I love watching.

And then, the next fight, you don't hold back. I see it coming the second my palm leaves your cheek. You don't hesitate. You hit me. Open-handed, mean, hard enough to make my teeth crash like cymbals, metal in my mouth, copper bloom of blood on tongue. And I grin. Split-lipped, stupid, half from shock, half from the cheap thrill of getting what I want. Finally. But it's there in your eyes, in the way you follow through. You aren't just hitting back. You are making a point. That you're the man. That your hit means business. That if we were trading pain, matching force, you'd always swing heavier, land harder. And then, like some rabid magician trying to top his own trick, you hit yourself. Once. Twice. Again. Your eyes are wide now, wet glassy, but your mouth has that same stubborn twist. The sound of your palm on your skin is different from mine—duller, deeper—but it lands in me all the same. So I match you, and hit myself—the first one making my vision jump, the second making my ears hum. By the third, we're in sync, a two-person drumline, back-alley symphony, rhythm sick and perfect. My cheek feels swollen, yours is blotched and hot. And we don't stop. Not till we are breathless, staring each other down like animals bleeding out on opposite sides of the same cage. And that's how it stays. Every fight. We go blow for blow. Me to you, you to me, us to ourselves. Keeping score. Matching each other's damage, like proof we are equals in madness. Proof we aren't afraid to go all the way, if it means not losing ground.

And then something cracks. Don't ask me why. Some fuckery with your uncle's funeral or your mother's guilt. So, on a trip to Varanasi, we buy it, the bell. Not temple-grade. Just brass dulled with age. Fit right in my palm. We kept it on the drawer beside the keys and the cracked image of the guruji your family swears by. We say we'll ring it when we are close to the edge, or beyond it. The ding ding ding means one thing—STOP. And for a while, it works. One of us reaches for it, the other goes still, the sound holding us in place like a hand to the chest. Dogs trained to the bell. It works, until it doesn't. Until we ring it too often. Ring it for show. Ring it to win. Ring it like punctuation instead of salvation. And now it just echoes.

Pointless. Hollow. A ghost clanging, ding ding ding. And still, we stay. Still swing. Still ring. Because the damage feels honest, and the silence after the bell? That's the closest we've ever come to peace.

*Fifth drink. Sixth. Seventh.* I don't know. First night. Back at your place. *Ssh … relax. I got this. I got you*, you whispered, smooth rehearsed, an order disguised as balm. It sounded less like comfort, and more like something once mistaken for kindness. But I bought it. Believed you. I'd been trained to reward effort. So, I opened, body before mind, and your mouth landed between my legs like a wet lie. And I let it happen. Not because I wanted to, but because I was too fucking drunk not to. Consent isn't always a simple yes or a no. Sometimes it's silence lined with shame, old bruises that light up under a certain kind of touch. Sometimes it's a freeze, a fawn, a forgetting. I told myself: This is okay, this is what wanting must look like, your lips in my cunt, and your hand on my tits, too fast too soon too certain.

Funny. Before I left, I promised myself I wouldn't fuck tonight. But I gave in. Maybe Ma was right. I am easy—a slut. But even now, this—*us*—feels like a crime scene I keep returning to. That night, the first one, clung; and this one, too, clings. Like an encounter with a man I thought I knew. *But I don't I don't I don't.*

A stranger you are—though the coming-together moment was real. So real, we kept it separate from everything else; from life, from love, and from consequence. Two individuals on a timeline that shouldn't have touched, but did. Nearly a decade of fooling each other and ourselves. A lifetime, it seems, pissed away. And all of it narrowed down to a single, suffocating room where it began. Your room. It was magic, sure. The sticky bar floor, your hand on my thigh, and the trail you licked down my neck. I whispered something like, *I want to sleep in this, wake in this*; and I did, until I didn't. And when I refused to give you the soft moan, the open thighs, the half-smile, you dissolved deeper into filth—the kind of pornography that eats at the last thing human inside you. I watched you become the man who didn't need connection any more, but still wanted control. The exhibiting nude—live meat for eyes. I didn't stop you. I didn't care. I witnessed you unravel, nude from behind the glass, stripped of everything soft. I watched, not with jealousy, but with grief. You humiliated yourself for dead-eyed voyeurs and for strangers with usernames that read like broken code. A digital slaughterhouse where nothing was sacred, and everything went. The first few times I objected. You laughed-shrugged and said, *you used to like it too*. And fuck! You're right. The thrill of doing it, side by side, high on Old Monk and ganja, taking requests, fucking wild things in front of blinking red lights, pixellated and blurred, was real. It was us, together, amping each other up, turned on by being watched, by being wanted, not replaced. But now. Now I wasn't in the frame. I wasn't even in the room.

You made a drink. You didn't check if I was watching. You just went on, full screen surrender, offering yourself up, looking for love in a chat window filled with emojis and half-sentences and low-res compliments. You looked for *me*, maybe, but only in theory. Because you weren't trying to fuck me. You were not even trying to find me.

And I?

I didn't stop you. I didn't interrupt. I didn't scream.

I just sat in the next room, headphones on, scrolling scrolling pretending. This one time, anonymous, I logged in, and watched you, naked, on our bed, taking requests, jerking off. I commented: *Hey, where is the slut, bring her back*. You ignored the message, and carried on. You used to say we were rebels, fucking on cam for the rush, the tips, the danger. It was love, once. I'd ride you with the kind of feral joy that made men jealous. Gods too. But now you did it alone—mute mechanical, a routine. Like brushing your teeth. I wanted to ring the bell, ding ding ding, but I didn't. Because I'd given up trying.

I'm no saint either. Never was. God knows I've screamed, fucked, lied, clawed. But I'm tired. Bone-tired. The kind that seeps behind your eyes and never leaves. I don't want to be your cure any more any more any more. I don't want to be your answer. I don't even want us. I want silence. I want out I want out I want out. And if I'm still here tomorrow, it won't be for you. It won't be for *us.* It'll be because I am waiting for permission. Because I haven't yet learnt how to vanish. But I will. Oh, I will. *Maybe.*

Remember how it used to be? The early years. Repeat? Yes. Sixty. Old Monk. Memory—it's a joke now, red-nosed and mean. Doesn't sting any more. From daily breakfasts, to meals over weekends, and the morning kiss—a ritual you called divine—none of this exists. No longer do we read poetry like we used to, and no longer do we read Reddit grief support posts. We nod. *Hmm.* And fuck like it owes us something. Saturday. That's the day. The marital grunt. Our holy sabbath of skin. Couples therapy bullshit.

*You comfy?* you ask, giving my nipples a half-assed lick, like you're checking a stamp for authenticity. I nod. *Hmm.* Because what else? The sheets are damp, tangled. The AC whines. The fan whirrs. A mosquito buzzes with a warning we do not pay heed to. You peel off my underwear like you're unwrapping disappointment. No music. No teeth. A dry kiss. No tongue. Missionary. The end.

And we roll apart. No cigarettes. No cuddles. I turn my face to the wall. You reach for your phone. It used to be tender. Then wild. Then brutal. Then sad. Now, it's just silent. Not peaceful. No. This silence is thick. Loaded. It says we've survived. Also says the things I have never said. I hated the way you left your socks under the bed. Hated how you cleared your throat. Hated how you always talked over me. Hated the way you said, *calm down*. Hated that your apologies came with a joke. Hated the way you said, *stop overthinking it*. Hated the sound of your chewing long before I hated you.

I checked your search history once. Never told you what I found. I fantasized about living alone every time I folded laundry. I was relieved the first time you went away on a work trip. I kept track of all the times you didn't say, *I'm proud of you*. I hated the smallness of my life around you.

I have stopped cooking our favourite meals. You don't notice. I say I don't mind you forgetting, that you don't even look at me any more. Your eyes skim, as if I am wallpaper left behind. And I hate you for that too. Not the loud kind of hate. No. Mine is quieter. More ancient. The kind of hate that waits, lingers and settles into your bones. The kind that knows your breathing patterns. That has memorized the shape of your back turned in bed. I hate the way your eyes flash pity instead of hunger. I hate the way your voice has turned careful, your affection hesitant, like I'm a wound you don't want to press too hard on. And I hate how you navigate me, like a haunted house, expecting something to jump out and scream. And even when I try to remember the happy times, I can't. The memory's been overwritten by repetitions—the blur, sweat silence, the hum of appliances, and your voice, low and empty, whispering, *ssh … relax. I got this. I got you*.

And I want to scream. Slap you. Ask: *Who're you saying it to, me or yourself?* But I don't I don't I don't. And still, I remember things. Like that one time, I dared you to try it, and you said okay. Strap it on. Shit. Piss. Smear. Make it worse. Make it unbearable. And I did. Not because I wanted to, but because I wanted to see how far we would go. And we went far, and they liked it, commented, more filth, more deep, more more more, please. I used to cry from the joy of it. You'd hold me like it meant something. Like *I* meant something. But that was another life, another us. I open my mouth like a grave. You spit—I swallow. I leak—you feed. Shame is honey—sticky sweet, tasty. Yum, I say, and you laugh, call me your favourite bitch. We don't blink, hesitate, throw up, or look away. We sit together because we love each other, still. Or we're here because we've got nowhere else to be.

And our resentment, black and thick, stews under our ribs. You call it passion. I call it mould. For the time being, we label it desire. It's just rot in lingerie pink. You pop the pill, blue like cowardice. I pretend I haven't noticed. We wait. The silence is *routine*. Like taking a shit. You know where to touch. I know how to flinch. We fuck like clockwork, erasing tick-tick the softness from our bones. *Ssh … relax. I got this. I got you*, you whisper. Holy goddamn vow. It lands like a receipt. I laugh, it's brittle. Those words used to mean sanctuary. Now it's a customer complaint on hold. The sentences are on loop. They break.

And me?

I'm fucking exhausted in the marrow; a biohazard with tits. Na—scratch that. I'm a stain. No, I'm more than a stain. I'm the whole fucking spillage. And I'm tired of being mopped up. If we fuck, it's because … what else is there to do? We're too chickenshit to leave. And when you finish, and I don't, I close my eyes and listen to the ceiling. It creaks like it's trying to escape us too. I ask: *If I vanished mid-fight mid-fuck mid-breath, would you notice?* Or would you keep going, chasing the ghost of me, pretending this is still mutual?

The silence after is louder than every fake moan I've ever gifted you.

I used to fake orgasms.

Now I fake sleep.

I fake not giving a shit.

And you whisper again, *ssh… relax. I got this. I got you.*

No, you fucking don't. But I let it pass. Let the lie hang between us. Because naming it would mean ending it. And I'm not ready yet. Not because I love you, but because a part of me still believes I deserve this. And that part? She's louder than the rest, for now for now for now. I fold into the night, into the sheets, and into the part of myself that folds too damn easy. And you sleep. And I don't. And the ceiling listens with me.

And when it gets quiet inside, too quiet, I wish you'd just die. Please. Die for me. Yes. I want you dead. Not out of hate, or love. No. But because death is clean. A white sheet pulled over everything we broke. No more door slams. No more half-fucks. No more Saturdays where my body's a chore and your cock an item scratched off; and no more crusty socks under the bed, and no more chewing with your mouth open, the wet smacks I hear in my skull at 3 a.m. No more pretending. No more explaining. And if you died, I could forgive you. Rewrite the whole mess in past tense: *We tried. We fucked. We failed.* And I could finally grieve like a good wife, forgiving all of our ruin. Head bowed, lips shut, palms pressed to a corpse that will mock me no more no more no more.

The thought first came like a flutter—a pillow hovering over your slack mouth in year three. You slept with your jaw loose, breath wet and whistling. Drool threading into the case. The fan moved like a metronome—*do it do it do it.* I imagined the soft press of fabric, quick, merciful. A dark joke in my head, half-giggle, half-prayer; the thrill of it, sparky, turned me on.

The years stretched the thought. Gave it shape. Edges. Scenes. Your death started wearing flesh. By year four, it grew teeth. You drank too much. Said something flat; surgical. I looked at the empty wine bottle in my hand and thought—*one good swing, and it's over.* Your skull split, ripe and gooey. Instead, I puked into the sink. The smell of bile, chicken and dish soap. Rinsed my mouth. Crawled into bed. And when you reached for me, I spread like a whore on call. I hated it. But I needed it too. Then I started collecting ways women kill men in movies. I noticed. Catalogued. Stored them like recipes.

Year six. Scene from a French film. Sleeping pills crushed, stirred into soup. The woman smiled as he sipped. I paused, rewound and watched the smile bloom in her cheek, felt it bloom in mine. Later that week, pharmacy aisle. Sleeping pills lined up like soldiers. A woman on a box advertising her lavender death. I want that silence. Didn't buy them. Just stood there and let the fluorescent hum buzz through my skull.

By year eight, the heat was gone. What replaced it was colder. More deliberate. I saw a film where the killer extracted cyanide from apple seeds. It was absurd. Slow. Meditative. Next morning, I caught myself at the fruit cart, finger tracing the waxy skin, asked how much for a kilo. Bought five. Let them rot for weeks, imagining your tongue, blue and quiet. Instead, fruit flies. Little black witnesses to my failure.

And now? The thought doesn't even feel like sin. It moves in. Unpacks. Lives here. I see you dead in every room—not bloody or broken, just still. Warm, breathless in the bath, the bed. Your chest rising—falling—stopping. Clean blessed, finished. I imagine calling someone. I imagine my voice rehearsing grief. And god, the relief of it. The freedom to love you again as memory, to hold your shirts without the weight of your scorn in the sleeves. *Darling. Die please. Just fucking die*. Not because I'm broken. Not because I'm crazy. Not because I'm that girl. But because I've run every other scenario, and this is the only one where I'm finally free without being punished for it. Because I've been polite long enough. I'll cry for you, if it helps. I'll write the eulogy, plan the funeral, won't remarry. I'll even forgive your mother, the way she smiled when she said I should be more like your cousin's wife. I'll wear white. I'll kneel. I'll perform. I'll bow my head and let the salt leak quietly through my nose. I'll say: *We had our moments*. I'll say: *He loved me in his way*. I'll say: *I was lucky*. And your friends will pat my shoulder. Your office will send condolences. My name will appear once in the obituary, right after *beloved wife*. And I'll smile, just enough, just once. Because it'll be over. And not because you left, but because I finally stayed gone.

I won't need to explain myself.

Not to the shrink.

Not to the next man who asks what I'm looking for.

I won't be looking any more.

I'll remember your shirts, but without the stink of garlic and forgetting. I'll remember the shape of your hand, but not how it hesitated—hovered—then claimed. I'll remember that first kiss, but not the way you kissed me like I was already yours. And when I come home, there'll be no socks under the bed. No fucking mouth-chewing in the middle of the night. No *hmms*. No half-fucks. Just me. Breathing. Ungodly, alive, untouched. And that, my love, is all I've ever wanted.

We are drunk, filthy in the way only bodies can be, after too many hours sweating in closed air, too many humid nights, and too much rum left sloshing in the gut. The walls hold heat, trapping it with the stink of sweat, sex that hasn't happened yet, and the sour bloom of liquor evaporating from our pores. The sheet clings to me. My thighs stick together, and I feel the crust of dried tongue where my breasts meet my ribs. *I'm not sure*, I say. Your mouth grazes my ear, the rasp of your breath hot chemical, laced with the rot of rum left too long in the glass. *Ssh… relax. I got this. I got you*, you whisper, pressing into me. I stare at the ceiling, a water stain shaped like a dog crouching to shit. Your hand moves between my thighs, nails dragging through stubble, catching on a pimple I popped in the shower. The stink between us grows heavier, a low tide stench of skin and spit and the metal bite of blood where I've bitten the inside of my cheek. And then, the NO comes, sudden violent, a spinal jolt, my thighs locking, a clamp hard enough to bruise us both. And you stop. Wait. Patient as winter. This pause between us is a joke—slapstick, pathetic. And yet, it's also a mercy. A moment of my choosing. I almost laugh, but I don't, unsure at the comedy that is me—a girl in 'woman moods' crawling inside a warm ditch. You try to ease me open, the patience of a man convinced he's taming a wild bitch. My fingers knot in the sheet, pulling the seam loose, nails splitting at the quick. I don't walk away. Not yet. I keep my knees locked, hips angled sharp so there's no way through. You press, looking for a way in, but my body holds shut, not trembling not pleading. A wall with no door. You grind against the outside of me, the base of your cock slick from spit. Not welcome. The heat builds where our bones meet, bruising deep, a friction that burns without opening. You approach again, softer now. *Ssh … I got this. I got you*. Your words sound like a prayer to a god drunk in the gutter. And I take them in, let them coat my mouth and swallow hard, feeling them lodge in my throat like a clot I refuse to cough up.

We're wasted; drenched in rum and myth, the make-believe, that this—here and now—could become something. So I stay. Not for love. Not for softness. But because leaving means giving back the body I've just reclaimed, and I'm not done with it yet.

*It's our first time.* I say *no. I can't do this. Stop, please.* And it falls between us, my refusal, shattering the air. Your body goes rigid, hard-on hanging like an accusation. And we loosen, piece by piece, bitter sighs unravelling. You step off me, careful, like I'm a shrine or a minefield. Sacred. Radioactive. Both. Neither. And *it's okay*, you say, *we don't have to do this*. Like you're offering mercy, not masking control. And your kindness is cruelty with sugar. I feel it down my throat, syrupy thick. Because now it's my shame, not yours, stinking up the room. I can't look at you any more, or myself, the skin suddenly wrong on me, slick with sweat and the trace of almost-sex, a wet echo of what didn't happen. Our naked bodies side by side are crime scenes waiting to be bagged. Twin disasters. Not guilty, but stained.

You don't say a goddamn word. I want you to drag us back, and shove us both past the point of sense, and tear the *no* out of the air, out of the moment, out of me—erase every polite boundary held through the night. Cross a line. Cross it. Cross me. Cross us. Show me the cost. Show me I'm worth it. Break something open so this night, first night, finally means something. I want you to meet the wreck I am with a wreck of your own. Meet me with something that isn't cowardice, isn't performance. But you don't you don't you don't. You reach for the lighter, steady, as if you've trained for this moment your whole life. Flame, drag, smoke curling from your lips. Then you walk the fuck out. No slammed door. Just the clean cut of absence.

And I lie there, sticky, a body unspent but used, like meat left out in the sun. Your silence. It has teeth. I can hear it saying everything you don't. *Ssh… relax. I got this. I got you*. But you don't say it. The retreat is a ritual, or a simulacrum of one.

And I've learnt you that way, learnt the map of your quiet, the drop and rise of your absence, the way a blind woman learns the depth of a stairwell with the echo of her toes. You don't have to speak; my body knows. And you want that. The knowing, without you having to ask for it. And I give—my compliance wrapped as care. And nailed into your silences, this: *Look at me. Look at what I carry. Look at what loving you has done to me. Look. Look. Look*. And god help me, I look. I fucking look.

But now, a decade in, I don't flinch. I catalogue. I remember. I survive.

Tonight, I can't stomach loving the two of you—the ghost who breathed lullabies into my hair, and this decade-old husk wearing your face. Or maybe I'll make space for both of you. Split myself in two—one woman faithful, bent and still, a vessel for your grief, and the other, a bitch with a jaw for breaking bone, who spreads for strangers, who sketches their faces, hunting for angles and shadows to ruin, imagining their mouths split, the bone white underneath, dragging those drawings into life, into sweat and skin and bite, until the fantasy has teeth. She whispers your name as she comes, a curse disguised as climax; letting the years of bile spill from her mouth, hot and bitter. The communion be damned.

And it makes me happy, that thought. And still, the guilt slithers in, whispering old catechisms: You owe him this—your flesh, your consent, your nights. To refuse is blasphemy. To deny, some ancient sin. So I agree. Saturday nights: fuck me fuck me fuck me. But now I say it like I'm loading a gun, not praying for rain. I lie back, spread, stiff and obedient. Be good. Be empty. A woman scripted. A role rehearsed. That's what love is. A giving without end, a swallowing of filth until you can't taste the difference.

But I taste it now. I taste everything. And I chew before I spit.

Year four: I remember the first time I said no. Not the shy apologetic kind, but a knife of a no, cold and glinting, meant to wound. It had weight. It had edge. And you froze, mid-thrust, mid-sweat, all ego and no exit plan. Left the room. Rage simmering under your skin, but keeping it civil for now. I thought that was it.

It wasn't.

The second time, you didn't swallow it. You shoved me, and it stole my breath, the room buzzy on its slow, ugly orbit. Your hands, clammy, closed on my wrists, leaving half-moons that bloomed purple. I screamed. Loud spiteful words that left scratches in the air, and you answered with a slap. My teeth met tongue. Blood, copper iron, childhood railings. And you saw it, and it shattered something in you. You crumpled, giving out, *fucking pathetic* knees to wood. *I'm sorry*, cracked out of you in loops. *I'm sorry I'm sorry I'm sorry*, a broken record begging applause. Like not killing me made you some kind of saint.

And I felt nothing, except a low coil in my gut—sour, brief—and even that didn't last. You begged, whispered things, blubbery, childlike, touching my thigh or my wrist like you were petitioning a god for mercy you didn't deserve. Your breath was old coffee and regret. I wanted bleach.

So, I turned it into a game. Let you think I was softening. Ran fingers over your hand like a *maybe*, and watched your eyes flare with infantile hope. And then I whispered—*no*. Low. Sweet. Cruel. Not out of revenge. Not to win. Just to show you—this?—this is a two-person trainwreck. We built it. Together.

And in that moment, I'd think about the smell of you after, the proof you'd leave on fabric, and how, like that first

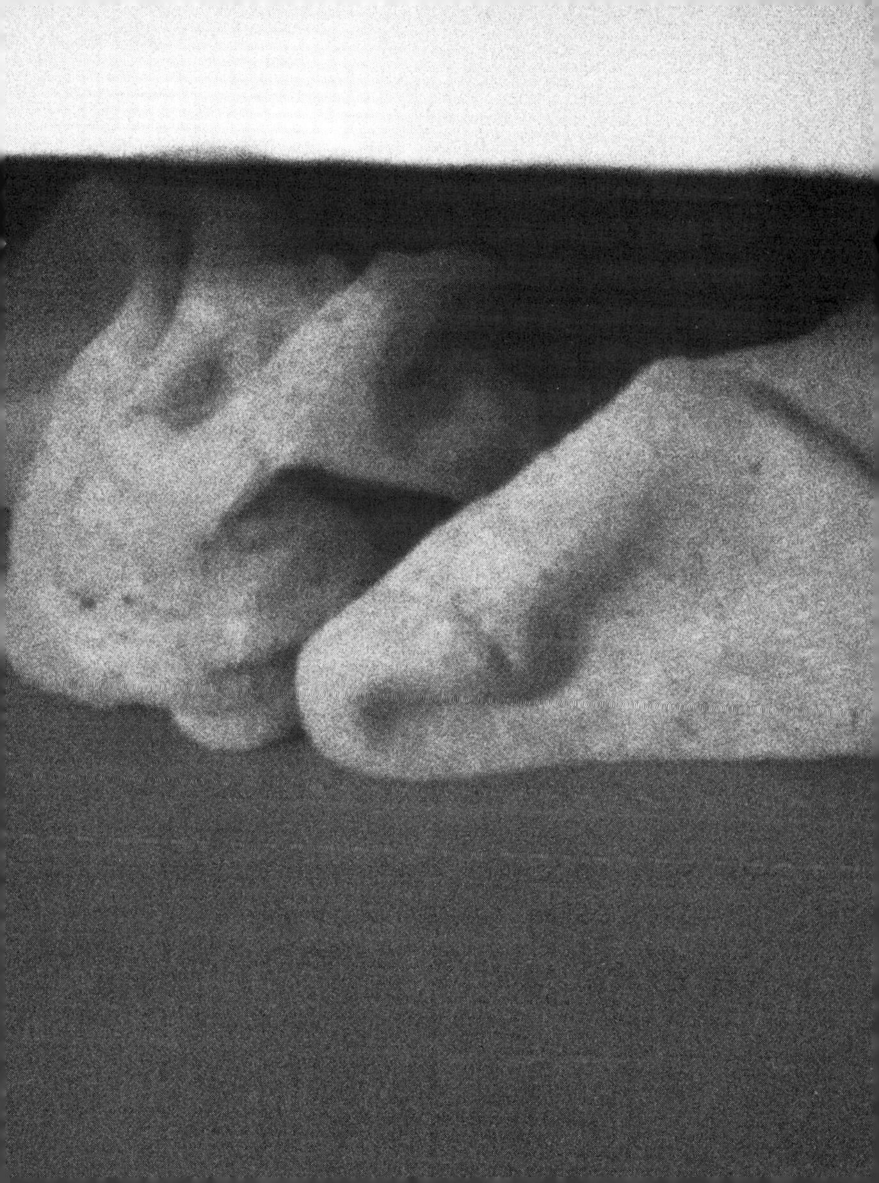

night, I might take it into me, not because I want you, but because I want the last word.

I don't forgive you. I don't hate you. What I feel is quieter, heavier—not vengeance, something purer, the pitiless satisfaction of a trap snapping shut on its prey.

And I give you permission you haven't asked for. I say: *Go cheat. Fuck someone else. Anyone. Pay a whore if you have to*. But you don't. You are too much of a coward. Too broken, too clingy, too stupidly loyal. And I savour it. The small cruelties. You, twitching when I raise my hand, though I do not hit. You, clinging to my breasts, starving thing, trying to nurse on memory, as if flesh can forgive. You, shrinking night after night, a man dissolving. Pathetic. And what're you going to do, even if I let you in? The pills blue don't work any more any more any more. Desire's just another dead thing on the table between us. So … what would be the point? Even if I opened up, whispered *yes*, you wouldn't know what to do with it. You can barely sustain *it*. Not for me. Not for yourself. Not for anything. I don't want to be wanted any more. I want to be understood and ruined properly. Or left the fuck alone. But no one ever leaves when they should. They hover. Like sickness. You're still here, pacing in the cage of what we built, hoping the walls will soften. They won't. I placed the bricks. Mortar mixed from every apology I swallowed before it formed. Every moan I faked just to get it over with. I didn't stop loving you. I started *erasing* you. From photographs. From the toothbrush cup. From towels I no longer wash with your scent in mind. I buy food that I like. I answer your questions with half-smiles and fractured verbs and *hmms*. You ask what's wrong. I say *nothing.* But I mean *you. Just you.* I want to burn the mattress. The kitchen. The skin I wore for you. I want to salt the earth of this house so nothing grows here again. Not peace. Not regret. Not memory. I want the bed to bite you. The doorknob to betray your hand. The floor to remember my footsteps louder than yours. I want to ruin you the way women have been quietly ruined for centuries, without monuments, without mercy, without a goddamn witness. And still, you ask if we're okay. Still, you think this is salvageable. Still, you look at me like a maybe.

I am not a maybe. I am a grave. And tonight, if I let you inside me, it'll be to bury you. I'll climb on top like a priest on a sacrifice, knees puncturing ribs, watching your eyes scramble for the man you thought you were. I'll take your wrists and press them into the mattress, until your knuckles beg for air. *Ssh … relax. I got this. I got you*, I'll say, *breathe*—not because it's mercy, but because it's the law. My fucking law. And I'll make you hold my gaze. Look what I carry. Look at what loving you has done to me. Look. Look. Look. And when you're looking, I'll say your name slow, syllable by syllable, until it feels like a sketch I can ruin, and flush. And when I finally let go, it won't be because I'm tired. It'll be because I'm done. I'll watch you scramble for your clothes like a dog dragging a broken leg, knowing I've made you smaller than the man who walked in—a bitch. My bitch. And maybe I'll do it again. Keep you here under my hand until the thought of me splits your sleep. Until you can't even touch yourself without feeling my weight. Until the memory of my voice makes you flinch in the shower. I don't want to haunt you. I want to infest you and rot the meat from the inside out, so you carry me until the day you die. And when you do, I hope you choke on it.

You suggested couples therapy. I said yes. Why not. And what did I get out of it? Saturday nights; a schedule for fucking pencilled in between work, laundry and groceries—precise-clinical-joyless. The shrink called it scheduled intimacy. I call it necrophilia with better lighting. And now, here I am. *On my fifth drink, or the sixth. Seventh.* I don't know I don't know I don't know. But it's nice, the not knowing.

It's our first time. I stay frozen on your bed, a stranger's territory. Sheets soft as sin, and ugly as hell. My heartbeat is a cracked drum. I watch the ceiling breathe, notice a water stain shaped like a dog crouching to shit, and I think, this is what survival tastes like—stale air, copper in the mouth and the faint trace of triumph. I lie to myself, *this is nice*, I say, *tender kind, gentler than most violations*. I should scream, but I purr. A mercy fuck dressed in soft lighting.

So why resist? Resistance is for girls with exits or options. I'm past the door, past the kiss and past the moment. Had ample opportunities. Should've left when you apologized to the rick guy. Should've left after we kissed. Should've, but didn't. In the cab, wrapped into your chest, I said again, *I want to sleep in this, wake in this*. My mouth was an invitation—wet, insistent, a dare. You tasted of Old Monk and calculation. The cabbie caught us in the rear-view, his eyes meeting mine for a heartbeat too long. No judgement, just a flat knowing. It lit something in my gut—not shame, but a filthy kind of pride, a pulse that said I could make any man consent. So, I climbed onto your lap right there, in the dark backseat, not because I was drunk, but because I was sober enough to know what I wanted—friction heat, the closest thing to vanishing without dying. You whispered, *wait*, and I hated you for it; hated that you could curate desire while mine came rabid, clawing at ribs, looking for the stud to hang the kill on. And I wanted you to match me, to hit back with the same animal need, not edit me into something digestible.

And when we finally made it to your place, we stripped and went at it, as if our bodies were evidence that needed to be destroyed.

You're gone. Cigarette smoke hangs in the air, stale and sweet, half-dead, stinks of us, old seed and wet cotton. The sheet's bunched under my back, damp from where you were, where I am. My thighs are still open, absurdly so, like my body hasn't gotten the message yet. It twitches, hums. Not with want, just leftover voltage. Ghost touch.

I said no. Not gentle. Not playful. A flat, sharp no. *I can't do this. Stop, please*. And you stopped. Grabbed the cigarette. Lit up. Exhaled. Left. You bloody stopped. Most men wouldn't. Most men would take the no as foreplay. Why did you stop? Why the fuck—did you stop? And now, I'm here in your bedroom. Naked, but not undone. Just unfinished, with a cunt that aches. Not in that *porny* kind of way. It aches like a door that almost slammed but didn't. Pressure with nowhere to go.

I should say sorry. Leave. Go back home. Sleep. But I'm too awake with shame, and not the kind you gave me. This is my own. Ancient. Feral. Rumbling in the belly.

I sit up. The bed creaks. My body hates me for moving. The room's all wrong now. Too quiet. Like it's waiting to see what I'll do next. And I spot them—your undies, crumpled by the bed, waistband twisted, still warm, maybe, and I reach down and grab them from our clothes, from the scattered debris. Half-shucked skins, trousers slumped, broken limbs, socks, bra and regrets, the wreckage of shared urgency, pathetic between two people trying too hard to feel something.

We kissed like amateurs. Ripped like addicts. Tongues tangled like wet paper. Fast. Ugly. Grateful. And this is stupid, I think, but I do it anyway. I hold them like they might flinch. They don't. They just sit in my hands, soft and lived-in. I press them to my face. Inhale. Exhale. Repeat. *I'll not flinch from the truth of you*, I say (I think). The smell isn't sharp or foul, just you—sweat, sleep and groin. The underlayer of a person. And I breathe it in, waiting for revulsion. It doesn't come. Instead, the heat in my chest swells. Not with lust, or sadness, but with something worse. Need.

And then, I lick it. Just once.

The taste is cotton and skin salt, a hint of bitter. I lick it again. Deeper. There's a mark, faint brown. Not dramatic. Just there, that holy smudge of shit shit shit, tender as a bruise, a punctuation with no syntax. And I bring it to my tongue, slow, aware that once I do it, there is no going back. I'll forever be the girl who licked your shit, and that's okay, too, I think, and I lick it, longer, patient. Hold it in my mouth. Let it sit there. Not sacred or profane. Just honest. It tastes like bone dust and closing doors, the underbelly of every *yes* I ever forced myself to give. And I think about all the times I've said yes when I meant no; the taste of every compromise I made and smiled through. Every moment I left my body because it was easier than staying in it. But this? This is mine. I swallow. Nothing happens. The world doesn't end. The sky doesn't open. I don't cry. I wipe my mouth with the back of my hand. My lips sting. I breathe.

Slow. Long. Hold. Like I'm here. Like I'm still here. Like this body belongs to me, finally, even in the worst of it. It made me happy, somewhat, that I could lick shit and not gag. And I think, when you come back in, if you do, I won't say a word. I'll let you do it, or I won't. But either way, tonight I crossed a line. And it didn't kill me.

And for a long time I lay in it—the guilt, sweat and scent of gunpowder and musk, the last traces of what could've been. Then something shifted. The shame twisted in my gut, turned. Why should I carry it for the both of us? Why should I kneel in your absence, and chew on your cowardice, when this body, slick and humming, is mine first, mine before it'll ever be yours?

So, I rose, legs heavy from rum and fatigue, and touched the wet between my thighs, my heat, the spit of life, and I smiled, I think, ready to lick the salt of my sweat, and crown myself in the glorious NO I gave you. The one that made you light up and leave the room.

I lock the door, gentle, quietening the click, and turn to the mirror, rust bleeding from its edges. My face floats there, warped. I lean closer, take inventory—my tits sagging, skin loose, nipples cracked and darker than I remember. My belly hangs forward, soft and folded, the stretch marks pale. There's a bruise on my hip in the shape of your hand. A thin scar runs along my ribs, a fresh scab where the razor bit too deep. I look at it, pathetically slutty and gloriously obscene in its ruin. And I know that any man would still take it. A naked woman doesn't need to be perfect. She just needs to be there. But I'm not there. I'm here. Present enough to choose. Aware that even with the stink of old sex on me, even with the sweat drying, I could still say yes, and make you forget everything else. I hate it, but I also know precisely how to wield it. And I step closer. Stare. Touch my reflection like it might recoil. It doesn't. So, I drag my wet fingers across the glass, leaving a streak where my mouth should be. A wound. A warning. My mark. I press harder, smearing, until my own lips blur into something unrecognizable, a woman I could either become or bury. But it's just me. Still me. Still here. Still *this*. The damage, some mine, some left by others who didn't stay for the aftermath. Cuts. Burns. Flesh rewritten, a map of injuries no one names. Cigarette stubs pressed into skin, each one a claim staked and abandoned. Souvenirs from lovers and strangers alike, both types fluent in pretending that nothing happened, and fluent, too, in leaving. Each scar says the same thing—you were marked, you were used, hurt in ways you invited, or didn't, or couldn't stop. Proof of my degradation. Proof that I let it happen. That maybe I needed it to happen. So, forgive me, my love. It's our *first time.* And I can't help it if my body shuts down. It has its own logic, its own traps, and an archive, older than the mind. It reacts before I can speak. Folds inwards. Hardens. Goes cold. Remembers every violation like scripture and obeys. And I see no beauty in it. Never have. Never will. There are people born into grace. My mother was like that. She had the kind of face that made men look stupid. She'd sit and paint herself perfect, while I watched from the doorframe, eight, maybe nine, already knowing I wasn't her. Would never be her. She told me once, *you have your father's nose,* as if she were naming a tumour. *Your shoulders are too wide: Hide them. You'll never be delicate. But you can be—interesting.* I was eleven. So, I learnt to vanish in plain sight, and to wrap myself in sarcasm, and clothes that swallowed my outline, and I learnt to loathe mirrors, while worshipping them in private.

And yet, you want this body? You reach for it. And that part knocks the wind from me. That you choose this skin, this ribcage with its old screams. Is it me, or just the rum, or the fact of the night, the thrill of fucking a chick on a *first date*? Or is it the loneliness curling in your belly? Are you that desperate? Am I?

You said, *wait*. Backseat of the taxi, jeans cutting into my thighs, seam pressing sharp as I straddled, hips grinding against fabric, ache swelling at the tip of my cunt. I wanted to tear them off, but your hand closed around my waist—*wait*, you said, voice low, eyes lit. *Not yet*. The words scalded. *Not yet*, like punishment. *Not yet*, like you wanted me trembling. So, I waited. Zipper biting, unyielding.

And here, in your room, I'm still waiting, confused hollowed with want and shame.

You touched me like I were a relic, and I recoiled. *Don't, please don't.* I flinched, the way people flinch from light. I want to let you in. But softness terrifies me. It's a leash braided from promises. And I know the trick, the leash tightens. I learnt that—men with gentle hands turn sour quicker than bruised fruit.

There was one such man, early on—eyes like lullabies, a face that could calm a riot. Brushed my hair as if it were the most critical job in the world. But when I said I couldn't sleep, he thundered. Said I was too sad for no reason. Yelled until I wept apologies.

Another one, older, beautiful in a way that made people stare. He cooked for me. Lit candles. Wrote poems that rhymed. Then one night, drunk and soft-voiced, he said I was lucky that he loved me because no one else would.

Then came the one who used silence like a scalpel. No yelling. No bruises. Just an absence so loud I could hear it in my chest. *But I never hurt you*, he said. *Yes. You never did, because you never touched me at all.* No messages. No questions. Nothing. I'd cry in the next room, and he'd play music louder. He loved me the way you love an object: Only when it works.

And the last one, the one before you. Kissed me. His hands never rushed. The voice never rose. But he needed saving, and I tried. Gave everything, marrow and light. And when I cracked beneath the weight, he fucked off without looking back. Said I was too much. Called me a bitch, spat on my face, and left. As if they didn't build me that way, all of them. Shovelled their need into me until I overflowed, then cursed me for spilling. So, you see? It's not that I don't want your gentleness. I just don't know how to hold it. Your touch makes me want to become worthy. And I'm afraid I'll ruin it. So, if I pull away, if I freeze, if I go someplace else mid-kiss—it's not you. It's just that, every time, softness arrived wearing a knife.

And they always leave. Once they've had their fill, they leave. It's the one truth I can count on. So, I said *no*—or some part of me did. Plus, you made me wait.

And now I feel your absence hot on the mattress, your ghost tugging at the sheets, fresh, still, the stink of you lingering like a prayer that backfired. And here I stand; wide open, naked in front of a mirror, your mirror—not sexy, or seductive. Just meat. *The moment's gone*, I say (I think). Doesn't matter any more. I mutter *fuck it*, reach for my clothes, and yank them on.

But my hands: They tremble. Shake. Hesitate. And that shocks me, because this body has always been game. Open-door policy. Let the wolves in. Lovers, abusers and relatives with father-eyes who should've known better. Fingers and fists, and commands barked, *good girl, bad bitch, bloody slut, hush now, don't cry, don't be dramatic*. So why now? Why the rebellion? Why, when I'm piss-drunk and loose, wrecked and ready to be nothing again, why now does my body buck like it's got something sacred left in it? What a fucking laugh. *Value. Worth. Dignity*. Cheap words for people too cowardly to jump. But maybe it's not rebellion. Maybe it's the final fuck you. A quiet little refusal that took twenty years to grow legs. A no older than some of the scars. Because saying yes was always easier. Cheaper than asking what I wanted. Cheaper than leaving.

The first one—the hair brusher, lullaby liar—he used to say, *you like it, don't you?*, while I bit my tongue to keep from gagging. He wasn't looking for a yes. He was looking for silence. Wanted to break the toy and still have it work. He tugged at my seams, bent me into shapes I didn't want to hold, testing hinges, just to see if I'd snap. And when I didn't—when I stayed—he grew bolder. Rougher. I let him, because why not. And then came the older one—the poet with his candles and casseroles, and a tally book. I found it once. Every refusal, a red cross. Every surrender, a smiley face. Said it helped in understanding me better, getting to know my rhythm. Said, *you always give in eventually. So why fight at all?* And finally, there was the fool who kissed my wrists. Called them his favourite part of me. Said: *This is where your life lives.* And I let him believe I was all silk and song. Docile. But I was a bitch, storm-born, wrecked. So when the muscle of softness gave out, and I snarled instead of cooed, he left, tidy as a folded shirt.

But before the exit, the erasure and tidy abandonment, there was the night. A nothing fight turned epic. I dropped to the kitchen floor, back against the fridge, clutching the old knife, whispering, *I want to die I want to die I want to die*. He paced, hovering, a buzzkill, lit a cigarette, inhaled and snapped. *Oh, fuck off with that shit. You want to die. Then do it. Fucking bitch*, he yelled, and took the knife from my hands, and kissed my wrists. And I thought, this is it, mercy, finally. But no. Instead, he looked straight into me, disgust curling, and said, *you want it that bad. Okay. Die.* And he dug in. Not a nick. Not a hesitant drag. No. It was deep. Angry. Decisive. Wrist to sinkhole. The blood came slow at first, a thick dark red, molasses-black. Then brighter. More insistent. It dripped down my sleeve and soaked the floor. I felt the warmth of it, the weightlessness. I tilted, and the room tilted too. And he didn't look back. Just grabbed his bag, spit, muttered *die* and left.

I don't remember calling. Just that I did. Somehow. My voice must've reached through. An old friend picked up and heard the apocalypse in it. Screamed into the phone.

So yeah. My hands shake now. Because they fucking remember. Not just what was done, but what I allowed. What I called love because no one taught me better. What I called sex because pain was familiar. These hands, these traitorous, shaking hands, they finally said enough. And maybe that's a kind of salvation. Or maybe it's just what's left after yes rots away.

The hospital was strip-lit hell. Nurses barked questions. One held my wrist, brushed with antiseptic, while the other stitched the wound, needle punching skin. I screamed. *Get the fuck off me. Just let it bleed. I don't want it fixed. I don't want to be here I don't want to be here I don't want to be here, please ... let me go.* But they just tightened their grip and kept at it. Then the doctor walked in. Clipboard in hand. Glasses too clean. Said: *We can find someone for you to talk to.* And I lost it. *I'm not sick*, I said. *I'm just done. D-O-N-E. You hear me?* But they kept going, talking soft, offering pamphlets, gentle nods and prescriptions. I spat at the floor. You're not saving me. You're just delaying it. I remember looking at the nurse's face and wanting her to hate me. But she didn't. She just looked tired. I was tired, too, but not dead. Not yet.

Now there is a scar. Snakes ugly on my wrist. Crooked. Loud. My relic. It itches when I drink too much or remember too hard. But it's mine. My battle ribbon. Proof I didn't vanish quiet. And every morning I touch it. Not gentle. Just to say, *yeah, fucker, still here*. So *tonight,* when I've left for the first time, this isn't rebellion, or defiance; this is just a body dog-tired, finally recoiling. This is rot, and rot is honest. It means something once lived. Something once mattered. And I see it—the girl on a first date, in your room, half-dressed, half-vanishing in a mirror, idiot enough to wait for you to come back. To say: *Ssh … relax. I got this. I got you.*

But you didn't.

So, I kept staring at my body. This carcass of me that never learnt worth; never learnt how to say no with conviction, only with curled toes and eyes closed. Born raw, twitching, open casket. Thirteen, in a stairwell, friend's older brother saying I looked like my mother, kissing me into visibility I didn't know how to refuse. Seventeen, moaning too loud, too soon, not from joy, but urgency. Get it over with, because no one ever told me my pleasure mattered. Twenty-two, waking in a stranger's bed, him already dressed, asking for his shirt like I was housekeeping. No name. No good morning. I smiled like I was in on the joke. And yet, I kept giving—not for love, not for coin, but for something colder, that cruel bastard currency: the permission to exist.

That first night: I walk out the room. Possessed. Not vulnerable. Light on my feet, naked, but not naked, my skin a different kind of clothing. You're by the window, cigarette burning down, ember glowing, smoke curling around your wrist like a lover that stuck around, a memory that forgot what it came for. Some kind of ghost with teeth, an absence pretending to have shape. I watch you from the doorway, the way your body surrenders to the night, leaning, unguarded, as though it wants to vanish in the dark. And I get it. I want to vanish too. Maybe into you.

Maybe away from you. Maybe both. The difference blurs. Desire is a trick: shifting, double-faced. I move towards you, not with grace but with inevitability, tide returning the wreckage. You don't turn right away, but I know you feel me. The air changes. The static shifts. You flick the butt into the dark. And I take your mouth. This feels right. Ash-flavoured, bitter, and maybe with a hint of grief. Perfect. We kiss like wounds that refuse to grow scabs.

This feels, for a stuttering moment, like resurrection.

But no. It's not new. It's never new. It's just the same ache wearing a different face. Still, I press into you. Still, you let me. There is no tenderness at first. Just need. Just the desperation of skin remembering skin, my hand in your hair, tugging, not gentle, but enough to make your breath catch, enough to remind us both we are alive.

You fall back into the chair, and I drop to my knees. Not as an offering. But as a threat. Face-first into you. No ceremony. Just dark warmth. Sweat. Salt. Memory, and a hint of death. I don't play pretty. I am one of those soft-porn daydreams. I go for it, mouth open, tongue working in slow, greedy strokes. You cock's half-hard, tastes like soap and yesterday's sins. And I want all of it—the piss and the promise, the stink and the sweetness, and the god rotting in your pelvis. You groan, low and startled, half-choked, your hand fists in my hair, not steering, just holding on. My tongue works, mining for truth, for sorrow, for whatever it is you've inside of you. The moan you let out is a crack in the world, ugly and desperate. I press harder. Lick slower. You shake. Curse. Your thighs clamp around my head, cage me, as if afraid I'll escape. But I don't. I never do. I let you unravel. Collapse. You sound like you're dying and being born at the same time. I don't choke. I don't ask for thanks. I just take all of it—the noise, the ache, the last of you. You are shudder-sobbing, teeth clenched like you're afraid that if you let go, you'll disappear completely. And when you come, you bury your face in your hands. Hide from it. From me. But I stay. Mouth wet. Face raw. I stay. I always stay.

You ask, *was I good?* And I nod, liar saint dog at your feet. I crawl into your lap, burying my face in the hollow of your collarbone. You fold your arms around me like we didn't just do something terrible and beautiful at once. And here we are, new and spent. The night leaks out of the window, black blood dripping, and I close my eyes. I do not know love. I do not trust love. But your breath is warm against my cheek, and for a moment—a small insect moment—I'm not afraid. Not of softness. Not of the silence. Not even of you leaving. Because right now, I'm here, my body whole. That must count for something?

And since that first night, I've been feeding you. You fucking hear me!

I've been feeding you like a mother feeds a dying child, like a whore feeds a man's ache, like a priestess pressing flesh into the mouth of a horny god. I gave you balm and marrow, broth and the fucking miracle of me. You flourish on my ruin. Grow fat off it. Happy in your way, like a man who doesn't know where the blood came from, just that the steak's still warm. Don't deny it. Don't you dare. Even in our mess, our fumbling, there is something close to joy. Sharp. Quick. Gone. But real. It sticks like dried blood under my fingernails. You know it. I know it. And that knowing; that raw, mouth-breath truth, damns us worse than anything else ever could.

I'm in love with a version of you. I'll be in love with it for years to come. We are together, and yet not. We orbit. Fall into bed. Wake up. The quiet stretches. Hours limp and useless. Deadweight time. And then only sweat, silence and the ache of being tangled in exhaustion. Nothing much occurs. We wait, and the waiting is a moment I carry, a softness that lies, pretends it can last. It can't. It won't. And it's not the sex. You're good. But I've had better. What has made me stay is the way you look at me, like I matter. Like I am a cathedral, not a crack-house.

And it makes me belong for one terrible instant. But it runs out. The warmth curdles. The gaze flickers. And all that is left is the slow choke of happily ever after. Not tragedy. Just routine. A Tuesday. But for now, we're enough.

Repeat.

Yes. Old Monk, large.

Lethargy came over me, over us. That's what killed it. Not rage. Not betrayal. Just *tired*. Lethargy with teeth.

And when I couldn't think of what to say next, I left. Got into the car, and drove. No music. Just silence and the sound of my rage chewing through the upholstery. *Don't call me*, I said.

What I meant was: *Say something. Anything!*

Nothing.

Okay. I'm putting it on. Do Not Disturb.

I meant it as a threat. It came out as a plea. You caught that. And still, you said nothing. Usually one of us cracked, gave in. That was the unsaid ritual carved into bone.

Tonight, no one says a thing. Rule broken. Covenant ash. And I beg with my face, my heat, my fists. Trembling. Look at me. Look. Look. Look. Give me your eyes, resentful and red, brutal, but look. You don't want to do this. I don't either. So, look at me. Please. Am I not even worthy of your gaze? We deserve to be saved. I deserve to be saved. Don't I? Don't we?

Nothing.

You stay nailed shut, coffin-tight.

And here we go again. What a fucking pussy. You're crying. And I don't care. Not tonight. I am too tired. Too used up. Too done. I can't wish away your grief, kiss the salt from your face. I don't have the energy, and I don't want to. *Sorry*, I say (I think). And I leave. Slam the door shut, a period punched at the end of a long, drunk sentence. I leave behind the debris of white dishes with flowers, baby pink green and blue. I have smashed a pair of our favourite coffee mugs. I leave the French press, and curtains ripped from rods, and our books of poetry ripped apart, Bukowski with Mary Oliver Plath Kamala Das Chughtai Faiz Ada Limón the love sonnets of Ghalib Faraz. Unbound pages scattered like the bodies of men and women who have fucked and forgotten. Like me, like you, like our gutted marriage.

Here's the math. Marriage is subtraction. You start whole. And then comes the taking—a slow striptease of self. Happily, at first. Like two dumb animals in heat. Then slower. Uglier. Each compromise—a lie dressed as mercy. Each kiss hides a blade. And someone always walks away with more. Someone walks away with nothing. That's the truth. The flesh knows. The soul pretends not to.

And I?

I know which one I am.

And I stay, still.

The fucked-up part? I miss you. And worse, I miss the stupid bitch I am when I'm with you. Soft. Spineless. Some half-lit creature alive in ways electric. Heart turned to pulp. I hate her, and I want her back. Both at once. *Don't do it. Don't do it. Don't do it.* But it has been done now, and it's official too, a new scar punctured into our skins—date, time, fresh red, the autopsy of which will become a tool for future negotiations; the fights, many still to be had before we part ways for good, so broken, so beat, so debrised that not enough pieces of us will remain for anyone new to enter our lives. I like that thought, honest as a good fuck. It comforts me. And at our divorce proceedings, nostalgic-soft, you'll turn to me and say, *remember that night, if you'd said something, anything, we wouldn't be here.* And I'll laugh, reply, *you could've said something too*. And you'll say, *I'd have said something ... had you stayed ... but you left. Slammed the door. Hard.*

Outside, the neighbour ghoul, brittle bitch, with her dead-fish eyes, watches me leave, antennas twitching, a cockroach alert for gossip. She'll talk. They'll all talk. The old crows with turmeric breath, flapping their gums, feeding on my ruin.

Fuck 'em. And let 'em talk. Let 'em laugh. Let the whole goddamn world laugh. I have been honest, and that's more than most people can say. And that's enough. Let her listen. These walls have never held shit anyway. Not the screams, not the sobbing, not the good fucks or the bad. Everything swallowed up. Nothing left. Nothing sacred.

*Drop dead*, I say (I think). She opens her mouth like she might retaliate with something mean or poetic or motherly or sharp, whatever she thinks will slice. But I look at her, cold-slow, like eyeing vermin. She gets it. Shuts up. White flag silence.

Peace, at last. The kind you only get when you burn the whole thing down.

I take the stairs, every slippered step slicing through the tension, rubber soles skidding on old marble, veins green, bad karma, echo echo echo, ricochets, gunshots in my skull, a firing squad, the verdict stamped: Guilty as fuck. We've crossed over, moulted into the next phase—our love, our romance, our life, whatever the circus has been, not just dead but desecrated, a twitching corpse begging for mercy or a bullet, whichever comes first.

And through all of it, she hears. The neighbour aunty. Second-floor sentinel of suffering. Old bitch prophet with a gold nameplate, custodian of morality and a thousand complaints. Our witness our spy our chorus. The walls leak paper-thin, and she laps up every drop. Knock knock knock knock, three short, one long, a pagan drum, summoning gods of regulation and sin. Once, she even threatened to call the cops, said she heard domestic violence, like she'd finally caught us in the act. But what she didn't know—when my nose snapped under your hand, sick wet crack, you were bleeding too; your forehead pouring red from the heel I hurled across blackout-dark, rage-lit screaming. I am not your mother, not your saviour, not your fucking punching bag. No more no more no more. She didn't get that part. They never do. They want categories, binaries, the clean gospel. The man—bad. Woman—sad. The villain and the victim. The asshole and the bitch. Good. Ugly. Digestible. Neat stories they can retell over sweetened chai and biscuits. Not this mess. Not the sweat, stink or blood mopped in silence at 3 a.m. Not the bodies that shiver with want and fury and guilt. Not the kind of pain that keeps echoing through the floorboards long after the bruises heal.

But I?

I see it; claim it.

Every drop of blood mine. Every scream mine. Every silence mine. I'm the monster the villain the asshole. Me me me. And you too. So let her knock. Let her whisper. Let her light her incense and dial the fucking cops. Because this air swallows everything, blood grief orgasms rage, and yet I remain, clawed raw, alive.

Later, I stand on the landing. Railing cold on my spine, cracked tiles biting my soles, nose bleeding, breath shallow, cursing my tears, too generous, whoring themselves out for nothing. The corridor reeks: cumin, rot, Lizol. There's a hive overhead, fluorescent drones, insect wings caught in eternity. And I think: *how, how much, how much more can I scrape out of this ruin? How many mouthfuls of cunt, blood, rags, how many more lethargic fucks, before I am bone*? Then you appear—barefoot, slick, shirt plastered to your back with sweat. Shame dripping. *Sorry*, you croak, thick-desperate, an apology swollen with phlegm. *Please come back in. Don't make a scene. She'll hear*. The neighbour bitch, hag sentinel. Always lurking. Always sniffing. *Come on, babe*, you say, softer now, a coaxing. *I am sorry*, you repeat, again again again, as if repetition is resurrection.

And I?

Like a dog with a broken spine, I drag myself into your arms. I hate it. I crave it. I give in. And you pull me close; rough, then soft, false-tender, the way you always do when you remember I can leave. Arms locked, breath sour, sweat-salt filling my mouth. And I hate how good it feels. Hate how my body, shameless betrayer, curls into yours like it never learnt refusal. And there, in the stink of you, the crust of blood under my nose, your stubble grazing my skin, there's peace—so grotesque, so stupidly *human,* it makes me want to howl. But I don't. I stand there, nailed between love and fury, drip-drip-drip, a metronome for madness. A lullaby for the already-dead.

The butcher hugs the carcass. The carcass sighs.

We were legends once. That's what they said about us. Rebels, the perfect couple, the blueprint. And we wore it until it sank into the marrow, a crown, weight grinding bone. We outlived the myth. Became something too ugly for epilogues.

Soulmates. Marriage. Happily ever after. What a farce! It's just me now. Alone. Driving, engine snarling. No music. Speeding, as the city unfurls. Streets peel open. Pavements slick with oil and piss. Dogs prowl under broken halogens, ribs sharp as prayers, and trucks moan past, thick and low, a lullaby some would find comfort in.

Eleven missed calls. You. Still. Saved as *Darling.* A name that feels like a mockery. Each call a green spasm on my screen: begging pleading, pick-up please. The frantic vibration, a dying heartbeat in my palm—your heartbeat.

And I see you—sweating, pacing, the phone in your fist, muttering: *This is it, this time she's really gone.* You picture me hanging. You picture me splayed. You picture me stiff, mouth slack, wrists open like rotten pomegranates. A car crushed into a divider. Pills fizzing my spit. Dead, glorious, the way women must die. Pretty. Poetic. Wearing kohl. And god. That thought makes me smile. Not with joy. Not with revenge. Just—the deliciousness of knowing you're choking on dread. Because with each ring-back, you are shitting yourself. So this time, *Darling*, I win. I win by letting it ring. Should've opened your mouth when you had the chance. You didn't. So I bolted. Ring—ring—ring, green pulse flickering in coffin-darkness.

I keep driving. A vein split open, bleeding light into the guts of the night. A city too bloated to sleep. My hands clutch the wheel, knuckles bone-white, the engine seeping into me like morphine, a steady narcotic. Dogs howl, I think, or is it my ribs cracking open? I hear my mother's voice, punishing like a whip. There are auto drivers, zombied, beedis glowing like insect eyes. And girls, tight and sharp, thighs lit under smoggy lights, waiting for salvation in backseats. I know them. I am them. I was them. Will be them again. A ghost in heels. A ghost in jeans. A ghost with cunt for currency.

So, spend me, *Darling*. I don't break easy, not any more. I just bruise where it doesn't show.

A couple argues. A child curls under tarp. It stinks of petrol and slaughtered dreams. I laugh. Or maybe, I don't. Out here, hope is exhaust smoke. And your calls keep buzzing, venom under my skin, maggots crawling, *Darling Darling Darling*. Your dread a thing of vibrations. Get this: I'm not looking to die. Not yet. Not tonight. But I want you to think I might. I want your throat dry with fear—the image of me, phantom hanging.

So, I let it ring—ring—ring, until it feels like the city itself is calling me. Until I think, maybe, the streetlights are mouths, open and begging. And I keep driving into a scream. The city convulses. Lamp posts blur into spears. I want them to pierce me. I want them to make me holy the old way—stoned burnt nailed split fucked into silence. Foul freedom tastes cleaner than our love ever did. Out here, wounds stay wounds; no one dresses them with tenderness. Out here, no one calls it love when they mean control. Out here, the silence is honest; it doesn't wear a lover's mask. Out here, I can scream without being told to lower my voice; the night swallows it whole. Out here, the apologies come without a *but*. Out here, no one fucks you just to win an argument. Out here, I am not punished for my softness, nor am I rewarded for my submission. Out here, the moon doesn't interrupt me when I speak. Out here, I don't have to earn my place. Out here, I am not your therapist, your whore, your penance, your ashtray. I am not a vessel for your grief, your failing erections, your dwindling faith. Out here, I am not your muse or your meat. Out here, I belong to no one. Least of all to you. Out here, it's okay to rot, to be useless, to be loud, to be sensitive, to be *too much*. Out here, I am the slut the corpse the car the city. I am not yours. Not theirs. I am the refusal to heal. Out here, I don't need to be chosen to be real. Out here, I can call the past by its real name; I can say it was a mistake, getting married. Out here, nothing is beautiful, and that makes it bearable. Out here, there is no forgiveness, only forgetting. Out here is the real *Darling*, too real, and there's no room for pussyfooting. Out here, I get to die a little without having to explain why.

So, fuck it. And fuck you. And fuck us. Let the phone ring. You don't get to find me. Not tonight. Not tonight. Not tonight. And I drive into the black belly, into the howl, and into my rehearsal for vanishing. And you don't get to be a part of it.

And then: Enough. The driving, the wheel, the pilgrimage to nowhere. Motion for motion's sake. No music. No witness. No god. Just the engine's death rattle and the ache, a barbed wire twisting up my spine, whispering buzzies *coward coward coward, do something, anything, do it, end it*.

So, I do it.

Kill the engine. Forehead to wheel. Static flooding skull. Inhale. Exhale. Repeat. *Return to the moment*, she said, the yoga witch purring in my ear, voice vanilla sweet; *find it—your centre your core your being*. And I see her—skin linen-soft, cheeks flushed with what looks like a life well lived. A quiet erosion sculpting her into something strangely elegant. It's charming to witness her shed a younger self for a creased one. Will I age like that too? I doubt it. I will rot—quick, feral, ash before silk. No grace, no bloom, just bone snapping. Meat gone sour. Blow off some bridge one night when no one's looking. Not tonight. But eventually. That's the real pose, a corpse. *Savasana*. The only practice I ever mastered. *Return to the now*, she whispers again. But what if the now is poison, sewage running into the veins, the IV drip of rust and blood? I am here I am here I am here. See. And the 'now' grins back at me, gums black, tongue dripping pus and honey. And I weep. The betrayal of it. Tears. Hot. Animal. Salty slime on my face. I hate it. I want to bash it out. Skull to wheel. Bash until there's nothing but red static. But I don't. I can't. So, I weep. Still.

And then, your memory worms in. That day, stuck in traffic—rain-razors across glass, horns screaming like animals, wipers dragging smears of grey. And me? Over the console, cunt thudding recklessly into your lap, knees digging. Your hands slipping up my dress and grabbing my hips. I breathe shallow. You snag. I grab your throat, choke it, tease, licking the tip of your tongue. And I feel it, your cock rising under me. I unzip you, fingers shaking, panties flung aside, and sink down like I am dying. The windows fogging over, turning us invisible. You bite my neck, teeth carving psalms. And the horn blares when my spine hits the wheel. I laugh. Keep riding, grinding with that slick wet rhythm born from hate and want and love. The car rocks. Holy holy holy. Hell hell hell. Both. Always both. A fuck, primitive and blasphemous.

A family watches us, mouths wide, children pressed to the glass. I wink at them. Let 'em watch. I want them to see, and gag on it—the sight of dick splitting heaven.

Now, that memory writhes, sweetness crawling with rot. That girl in the car, open wet laughing, is dead. Buried under silence. Yours and mine. I look at her now, dripping snot and salt on the steering wheel, leaking ugly. And again, I think, I want to bash it out. Skull to wheel. Bash until there's nothing but red static.

But I don't. I can't. So: I weep. Wanting to scream or shatter something. I wasn't supposed to break. Not for you. I'm furious that I let myself go, that I let you see me unarmoured. Furious that you get to keep that image in memory—my cunt, my laugh, my body, unashamed. I want to erase it. Say: *I was never yours. I never will be.*

The pain is back. Rat wires lit, gnawing, crawling up. A cocktail of desire and disgust, indifference maybe, and hate. You could've stopped me. Should've. But you didn't. You just sat there, mute and cowardly. So, I left. Slammed the door, slammed skull splitting bang, and I said in my head (I think): *Let it bruise—let it be. Fucking pussy.*

Now. Take it easy. Ready. Yes. Bar-Bar flickered the sign. I smile. Park. Walk in.

Inside, the air is thick as semen, tacky on the tongue. Cheap whisky, soggy peanuts and chips, vomit napkins, grease and piss, and burps, vanilla wet. And mercy mercy me—chemically sweet Chicken Chilli 65, red brown and burning. Mercy. Not redemption. And maybe for now, that's enough. Old Monk. Large. No ice. No mix. Straight down. Burn scald tits ache ribs glow grief kicks its shoes off lies in me home surrender freedom grace. Die live both. Perfect. Happily ever after. Repeat. No. Where was I? What. Repeat. Right. Large. *On my fifth drink, or was it the sixth. Seventh.* I don't know. But it's nice, the not knowing.

And now I scroll, past days—weeks—months—years—a decade, for that picture of you from archived time. Pre-marriage, pre-bullshit. You hated the lens, you hated being seen.

Your hair is a mess, the T-shirt full of holes, and an armpit bare and ugly. You aren't aware of me. I click. Refrigerator light spilling out in a sickly square, your face tilted into the cold, half-bent, reaching for milk, I think, or a pint. You look tired, sleep clinging. That moment is the truest version of you I have ever had.

And here it is—glowing in my palm. And I can't stop staring at it. It feels obscene, more naked than sex, confession, regret. Like a secret I shouldn't have. A part of me wants to delete it. But I don't. I just stare at you, hunched, unposed, mouth slack, looking like a ghost. I think, maybe this was always the truest shape of us. Not the passion, chaos or the myth. Just this—two animals caught in the light. One stealing. One unaware. But we're alive, still. Aren't we? Lie to me, *Darling.* Say that this isn't the end. That this night is a glitch. That the morning will come clean and we'll make it. Coffee. Curtains. Bandaged wrists. Say it. Please. What am I doing here? At Bar-Bar. I should go back. You should. I know. Take a sip. Never as good as the first one, or as effective. What was I saying? Yes. There it is. The bottle he pours from. I like how he grabs it by the neck—deliberate, merciless, his grip. Like the bottle owes him something. I ache for it.

There was a time you held me like that, brutal and reverent. Recognition disguised as violence. But it curdled. You changed. Became something uglier. Quieter. Your grip slackened. The claim withered.

Now you touch me like a bureaucrat—Saturday-night paperwork, strip insert collapse. Holy fuck, holy taxes. And you blame me for it, and I let you—because why not. You said I was too much too loud too fragile too sensitive too emotional, too everything. So, I folded, years on repeat, until I could fit into your palm, a matchbox of a woman. That's it. Now we are just another scream pressed into the pillow, another *I didn't mean to* that never meant shit.

That one night, *this memory*; your bush scratchy against my cheek, the bathroom floor a crust of piss and bleach. And me, kneeling, gagged, lips stretched into service, as you leaned back on the porcelain throne, smug, eyes heavy-lidded, drunk on the theatre of it; your fingers hooked in my hair, yanking jerking, puppeteering my skull. I remember the stink—cock musk, ammonia—and my spit slack and stringy like yolk. It made me want to vomit. But I didn't. I took it. I always took it. It was the way our love was. *Is.* Bastardized and mutilated into obedience. That's what you wanted, isn't it? Obedience as liturgy.

Then, you noticed my hand, stained blue from a busted pen that had bled into my jeans, ink leaking. And you touched my fingers, kissed the tips, tender, mocking, soft as a taunt. *Looks like scrambled pussy,* you said and laughed, reeking of beer-arrogance. I laughed too—because why not.

*My turn*, I said. Quiet, certain. Waiting. Wanting the seat. But you didn't move. You never moved. You smirked, lazy, lips wet with beer, and tugged me up instead, dragged my body forward, grabbed my ass, and shoved your mouth in my cunt. Fed like I was just a vein you could tap. And even then, you faltered. Tongue circling, shallow, hesitant flicks, licking at absence, not the flesh, never daring to sink into the meat of me. That's no way to eat pussy. I wanted you to kneel. To worship. To kiss from the ground up, work

your way from my feet to my thighs. I wanted to press your skull in and choke you the way you choked me. But you stayed outside the threshold. Never gave me that. Never knelt. Not once in a decade. That was reserved for me—the dumb slut who said yes to everything. And worst of all, the climax never came. You kept me open, raw hungry unfinished, because that's how you liked me. Dependent. Half-fed. A cunt *almost there,* but never quite. And that's when I knew. You didn't want a woman. You wanted a mirror. A soft thing to reflect your glory back at you. And I gave it. For years, I gave.

Year one: floor mattress, dust motes, stuffy lungs, light like fish scales on the wall, your laugh. I thought: *This is how a room learns my name.*

Year two: We fuck on cam, tips, chi-chings, later, sink water warm, a plate slips, the apology in my mouth never spent, humming, I swallow, it breeds.

Year three: I don't sketch faces of men any more, feels like cheating, bathroom tile on my kneecaps, steam takes my face, gives it back wrong, I learn the trick of leaving my body standing while my body kneels, devotion in teeth marks. I want you to die. Afterwards, I rinse the red and call it ordinary.

Year four: Wardrobe air sick with our clothes. I hang the soft version of me on a wire and close the door, she drips. I dress in the one that doesn't cry any more. Later that night, I say my first no.

Year five: You jerk off on cam, they say bring back the slut, I wait for you to ask me, you don't. I step into the balcony. Ash rain, monsoon makes a throat of the city, I lean over the rail until gravity speaks. Plants dead again. I tell the body, not yet, it waits, patient bitch.

Year six: Bed seam down the middle, your back a locked door, my hand hovering at the hinge for months, I rehearse not-touching until not-touching is touch.

Year seven: Five sets of plants dead, *fuck it*, grocery aisle, milk and betrayals. I put peaches in the cart, bruise them with my thumb. Sweetness can rot. So can I.

Year eight: Mirror over sink, my tongue tastes of tin, old lightning, kept storms, I masturbate to the memory of us.

Year nine: Saturday schedule, intimacy stapled to calendar squares.

Year ten: The hour after midnight, I catalogue, see stars through the rafters of my chest, I drive, I howl into the dark, I need to fuck.

Now: Bar glass sweating, phone face down, your name *Darling* bright, I press my pulse to the rim and drink until the future blurs to a single syllable.

Also now: I tell the dark—*I am here, count me again.*

Inventory final: a mouth that can bless or bite, and knows the difference. And when morning happens, and it will, I'll name myself aloud, walk past our bed, and if you ask what we are, I'll say *finished*. You'll say *sorry*, I think, when it's safe. Clean. Forgive me, please. And I'll reply, too late, *Darling.* Too. Fucking. Late. And you'll stare at me, wet mutt eyes, pleading. Okay. Two things. Two. You nod fast, anything anything. One. I want you to get plants for the balcony, bougainvillea, white, pink, and I want you to water them, take care of them. Make them bloom. I will. I will. Promise. Two. Get on your knees. What? You heard me.

On your fucking knees. Just once. Just once in your whole goddamn life, descend. Lower yourself. Be the bitch I've been. Crawl for me, spit your jaw on the tile. And eat pussy like you're supposed to eat it. Properly. Not the coward's tongue circling around absence. Eat like you believe in it, until you choke on my glory like I choked on yours.

But you won't.

You were never built for reverence.

And still, some godforsaken part of me believes that underneath, something gentle survived. Some tender, pulse-beating truth. That maybe tomorrow I'll wake up and the light will be different, and you'll hold me whole.

And now, I sit here watching bottles breathe better than we ever did. Still. Aligned. Geometry perfect in their distance. Soldiers in glass skins. Obedient bastards. Except for those two, tucked in the corner, leaning. Close. Too close. Rebels. Traitors. Lovers maybe. Or liars. Bartender. Oye. Listen. Look. Those two bottles. They're too close. They're breaking the rules. See. They're not maintaining proper distance. They touch. Sweat together.

They've grown a sheen, wet glass slick like thighs under summer sheets. Dripping into each other. Whispering. Scheming. Like we used to. And I hate them for it. Their condensation becomes breath, their tilt, a secret, their closeness, an accusation. A crime against distance. Against safety. Against the death we agreed to. They're alive, these goddamn bottles. More alive than us. And here I sit. Wondering.

You know, this one time, I saw a reel. Instagram, late into the night. A girl with soft eyes, smoky voice, said people don't want marriage for love, not really. They want proof. A witness. A person who sees their life; who catalogues their cunt-stink mornings, stupid shit, the collapse on kitchen tiles, and the laughter that breaks into grief. Someone to confirm it happened. That they *happened*. That their ache wasn't wasted, and their joy wasn't an accident. That they mattered, once, to one set of eyes. And it makes sense. Marriage as archive. Memory. A paper trail of *having been*. And that's what I miss. Not the fucking, not the rush, not even the violence masquerading as devotion, but the gaze. The eyes that pressed me into existence and hammered me into flesh. Undeniable. Without it, I begin to turn into a ghost. A woman unwitnessed is a woman erased. Maybe that's all I ever wanted—someone to hold my mess to the light and say: *It happened, she happened.* Funny! How we mocked them, the couples with dead fish eyes in cafés, chewing silence, scrolling separate voids. Matching slippers. Matching keys. We spat contempt at their rituals, their pale routines. Called them corpses. Promised we'd never become them. That was our arrogance. Our rebellion. Soulmates. Special. Different. Fucking idiots. Because in the end, that's exactly what we became. Witnesses without testimony. You looked at me, until you didn't. And I went on existing anyway, screaming in silence, wet rot behind wallpaper. Ugly invisible inevitable.

And the proof?

It was everywhere, crawling in the small, stupid details. Like the pink Hello Kitty slippers we bought as a joke, the mindless joy of sinking my feet into them. But jokes putrefy into rituals. Rituals calcify.

Leftovers reheated four days in a row. Sex stapled between calendar slots. The Bluetooth speaker in the bathroom playing lo-fi jazz while we shit in sequence, two bodies synchronized in their banality. The groceries ticked off right. The way you start using a coaster. The toothbrush holder with separate slots. The drawer packed with takeout menus we never throw away, not for sentimental reasons, but because we're victims of inertia. Matching bathrobes. Your fucking Amazon order history. You calling me *babe* like it is a name tag. Beige. The death of red.

And we laughed at them? And then we became them. We became worse. Because we smelt the rot, and still, we swallowed we stayed.

And now we're nearly forty. No—forty-four. Forty. Fucking. Four. And this uneasiness won't fade. Rum should help. Blackout. Reset. But it doesn't work any more. Even the void spits me back out. I wake up, and the mornings don't forgive, don't fix anything. The light feels all wrong, and the coffee tastes like ash. Nothing makes sense. Not tonight. Not my hands, not your face, not the sound of my name in your mouth.

And yeah, I could have turned back—seen the exits, every single one lit in neon, pressed the brakes, taken a U-turn, gone home, knocked begged said *sorry*, meant it, turned small, licked your feet like I had that one time we fought, dropped to the floor, screaming through spit, *this is what you want.*

That time, you laughed. So, I remained gone. Too angry. Too bored. Too fucking *tired.* But there was a moment in there, right after the slam, and before the neighbour bitch came nosing in, a moment when I hovered outside, throat clogged with tar, too scared to knock, and too haunted to leave. But I did leave. Yes. I did. Because you didn't stop me. I drove, street into street, speedbreakers, slow-down slow-down slow-down, take it easy, turn left, fuck it. And before I knew it, the rhythm of the car, tyres on asphalt in that sickly orange glow, became peace.

So trust me, *Darling,* I wanted to come back to you. I fucking did. But you were effort. Yes. You, effort. You drained me. Sucked the youth from my bones. Wrung me into a rag and made bitterness my blood type. And still, I gave. A decade of cunt. A decade of silence.

The morning after that first night, my body raw, thighs wet. You, already awake, lit grainy-dim by the laptop glowing against your bare chest. Your face covered in eerie blue. I stirred, half-ashamed, half-curious, and asked, *what are you doing?* And you didn't hide it. Didn't snap the laptop shut or stammer. You turned your head, eyes gleaming with something wicked, solemn, reached out and wrapped your hand around me, cupping my breast, thumb grazing the nipple that was like a punctuation. You pulled me against you, kissing my temple my cheek my open mouth, whispering: *Reddit. Grief Support.* You turned the laptop towards me, and there it was, confessions, posts, death, naked and laid bare. A boy found swinging from a fan. A mother gone in her sleep. A father with a bullet in his mouth. A friend who just stopped breathing. All their sorrow typed out in jagged syntax, sobs breaking through punctuation, death death death gushing in typos and fragments. *Read it to me*, I said. *Okay, this is a good one*, you replied, and read. And I listened, half-sick, half-aroused, and I thought, *this is prayer*.

*Move on move on move on*, I said (I think), and you snapped the laptop shut again, looked at me, and slid inside. And we fucked, turning loss into heat.

That was morning one. The first liturgy.

And then it became ritual. Coffee brewed. Curtains yanked open. Light barging in. Obits on the screen, read aloud, and mouths pressed tight, pyre ash. I'd recite the words in my chest, tears, breasts squeezed, suffering as lubrication, with each loss my hips grinding harder against you, and my cunt clenching heat. It was possession. A haunting. I'd moan in sync with imagined sobs, stuttered sentences, gasps, your hand on my back, the full stop anchoring me in place; your cock, the grammar; and our bodies, pages inked in stranger grief.

And we kept at it, until their ache dissolved in our sweat, until I couldn't tell the difference between their loss and our lust, until it all blurred into one long elegy written in spit, in cunt-juice, in the feral stink of two animals mourning nothing mourning everything.

It was perfect. And then, it ceased. Because you switched jobs. Earlier mornings. Faster exits. No coffee, no curtains, no more grief. No more sunshine fucking. Just you, tie crooked, mouth full of toast, slamming the door.

And now, it's just me. Alone. Phone burning my hand, bar glass sweating into my wrist. I scroll. Same grief, different usernames. Still frantic, still broken, sentences torn apart by sobs. But there's no heat. No body pressed against mine, no voice to read the words aloud. Just me, devouring it, waiting for the fire that doesn't come. I keep scrolling anyway. Past suicide notes, cancer diaries and car crashes. Past the wailing of mothers and the silence of brothers. I scroll and scroll until my horniness dries, and throat goes sore. Until ghosts crawl out of the screen and sit on my lap. And I don't fuck any more. I don't even touch myself. I just sit. Alone. Witness to strangers who never asked for me. Desecrating the ritual we once shared. Desecrating myself. And I read:

*I am losing it, I think. Something in me is missing. Or wrong. I don't know how else to say it. It's like he never existed. A room that's been emptied out overnight. No mess, or dust. Just the shape of where we used to be. And that's what scares me. It's not that I don't miss him. It's worse than that. My body is acting like he was never here at all. Like remembering him is something I'm not supposed to do. He died six months ago. I know that. I know the date. People remind me. The calendar keeps going like nothing happened. But inside me, there's nothing. No response. No echo of his existence. It's like my insides have decided he's not allowed in any more. Like remembering him is illegal now. I try. I really try. And when I do, my chest tightens and my skin feels wrong, like it's rejecting the thought. I feel like I'm betraying something just by wanting to remember him. I don't know how to explain that without sounding insane. There's just a blank where years used to be. Almost ten years. And my body doesn't recognize him. My heart doesn't react. And that terrifies me more than anything else. So I try to force it. I slap myself. Not hard. Just enough to jolt. Like if I shock my body it will remember. It doesn't. So I pull out a photo. His photo. I say—look. I actually say it out loud. LOOK. This is proof. That's him. That's us. But his face doesn't settle in my head. He looks like someone I'd met once. A blur. A stranger standing too close. My hands start shaking because if he's a stranger, then what the fuck is my life? Today I went through everything. Every photo. Every message. Voice notes. All of it's still there. All of it's useless. I keep his phone on. Charged. I haven't turned it off. Sometimes I call myself from it just to see his name come up on my screen. Today it didn't do anything. No feeling or ache. Just his name. Like data. Flat. Administrative. I think I'm losing my mind. My brain keeps telling me I made it all up. That the years collapsed into nothing. That intimacy was something I imagined. That I invented a whole person and then mourned him. I feel like I'm watching my own life disappear quietly. Like someone is deleting pieces of it while I'm still here. No big breakdown. No crying fits. Just things going blank. I can't afford therapy. I don't have anyone to ask this without sounding crazy. I need to know if this happens. If grief can do this. If forgetting like this is part of it. If memory can just shut down. Please tell me this isn't permanent. Please tell me forgetting doesn't mean it wasn't real. Please tell me I'm not disappearing too. Because if he never existed, then neither did I.*

And here I sit, sticky shaken, guilty. Not just for what I did. But for the way forgetting you turned me on. *Darling,* die for me, please. Die. So I can write one of these. Grieve and be done with it.

I wipe my hand on my jeans, a wet stain blooming dark between the seams. The car stinks of it, sex and petrol. And the faint tang of rust. I keep the post open, reread the lines: *My body is acting like he was never here at all.* The screen glows, a wound in my lap. I scroll again, hungry for more. Her grief is cleaner than mine. Neater too. She weeps in full sentences, even when she stumbles. I, in fragments.

The steering wheel is slick, like bone soaked too long. I grip it anyway, and imagine driving until the tank coughs empty, until the tyres shred, until there's nothing left but me and this dull ache. I stay put. I breathe. Inhale. Exhale. Repeat. Yoga witch purring in my ear, voice vanilla sweet, and I press the heel of my palm between my legs. I find the ghost of you twitching like a roach that won't die. Still there. Still mine. The phone buzzes again. Your name. I let it ring. Watch the letters blur as my eyes water. Not tears. Not grief. *Darling. Darling. Darling.* Salt on lips. Wet heat down my thighs. The engine hums, steady as a heartbeat. For a moment, I wonder if this is all I'll ever be, a woman in a parked car, moaning, then silent, jerking herself off to the memory of being remembered. And from the post, I recall the lines: *I think I'm losing my mind.* And I am, and she is begging still, *please tell me this isn't permanent. Please tell me forgetting doesn't mean it wasn't real.* And I want to answer her, write back. Yes, *Darling.* It was real. It happened. You happened. Even if it kills you, it happened.

But my fingers hover, paralysed.

What right do I have to comfort anyone? I, who turned grief into performance, and who made a mockery of the very tenderness she's desperate to reclaim?

So I don't. I just keep scrolling.

Bar-Bar blares, music throttled by the clang of glass, idiot hymns of drunks stupid enough to still believe in tenderness. I sit, listening for the ghost of mornings when grief was foreplay, until it wasn't. *Getting late, my love*, you said, showered and left, leaving behind your lime-scented soap, saccharine citrus masking what I'd lick clean off your skin. You replaced the sweat with fragrance, your body rewritten as hygiene.

Betrayal. That's what I taste now. Not salt or spit or you.

Betrayal: sterile and perfumed.

I'd curl into the sheets, bitter, and weep, mourning a presence dead, and not dead yet, a presence that was never really there. Then I'd fire up the laptop. Start working. Because what else was there to do? Because it needed to be done. You okay? Yeah. Repeat. Old Monk. Large. *Fifth drink. Sixth. Seventh.*

Where was I?

Yes. That U-turn not made, even when an opportunity presented itself. I didn't take it. Could have. Should have. But didn't. Why? I don't know. Maybe something in me wanted the wreckage to stand. *Darling,* what happened to us?

I am hungry. You must be too. If the door slam hadn't sealed it, and you'd stopped me, said *stay*, then we'd have driven to that late-night street where vendors line up, slinging egg bhurji for fellas working the graveyard shift. We'd stand, shoulder to shoulder, you licking grease from your thumb, me tearing bread with my teeth, yellow butter bleeding down my wrist, chilli-stung lips, beer still in our blood, bodies raw from the fight, but alive, always alive. We'd eat like beasts—no knives, no forks, just hands and mouths, stuffed with apologies, spit, blood maybe. Jaws sore from screaming. Your knuckles red from the door you punched. Still, we'd tear bread together, smile. Hell, we'd even feed each other a bite, and kiss. That was our mercy, not forgiveness. Never forgiveness.

But you didn't stop me. So, the stalls won't see us tonight, and the bhurji will turn cold on someone else's plate. And I sit here, *drink number seven or eight* clawing at my gut, and I can taste it, the onions, the burn of chilli on an already cut lip, the salt of sweat mixed with egg. I am starving. For food. For you. And for the stink of our hands and our unwashed mouths pressed together. I'd wanted that forever, made my peace with it—the filthy feast after the storm. But you killed it.

Can I get some fries? Sure. Salted or peri-peri? Salted is fine. Thank you. You like peri-peri. I know. And all these years, I've tolerated that godawful orange dust for you. But not tonight. Tonight is my kind of fries.

*Come on, try one, I promise you'll love them*, you said, your fingers brushing mine. And I picked it up, powdery dry, harmless, until it hit my tongue, and the orange dust rose, not flavour, but fallout, dry heat scratching, sandpaper down my throat. A cough begging to explode. But I held it. Because you were watching. Your eyes lit, waiting for me, and I forced the fries down, the grit, the raw sour-metal tang coating my insides. *So …* you asked. *They're nice*, I replied, a lie wrapped in salt and smiles, and reached for my drink, quick, Old Monk biting the wound shut, cauterizing the lie before it spread.

Do you know what it means to swallow against instinct? To gag and still push down?

Because I do.

And then it arrives, uninvited—piss blooming on clean sheets. A memory. Someone—an aunt, friend, therapist, a stranger with kind eyes—said, *have a child. It'll save you*. And for a moment, I toyed with the idea—a baby, a fragile placeholder, a wet scribble in the margins of our story. We'd take photos and share them on WhatsApp groups, or as profile pics, say *cheese*, *look*, *cute, isn't it*. And we'd become one of those couples we swore we'd never be. And we'd think, maybe this is enough. This is it. But slowly, inevitably, it would dull. We'd move from *can't believe we made this* to *why is it crying again? And again?* I'd look for you, but you wouldn't be there. You'd be gone, thumb scrolling, detached from the scene. You'd leave for office, tie crooked, deadlines spilling. I'd stay. I'd have to. Soaked in milk and shit and silence. A human bib. And I'd imagine the crib. And I'd see, not the child, but the outline of one. The empty weight of absence. Silence screaming louder than any infant's howl. And I'd smile. Always smile. And it would cry, demand to be seen. My mouth would say *sure* instead of *fuck off*. I'd be exhausted by it—my skin grey with fatigue, breasts leaking, tethered to feeding, nappies, and the drudgery of motherhood. I'd stink of milk and ammonia. My words would shrink. The body would disappear. And no one would be there to witness the slow erosion of me, no one but *it*—blank-eyed and demanding. And hate would bloom, unholy.

Someday, it would run a fever. I'd call you.

You'd talk to me, cold, in that tone, accusatory, *call the doctor again.*

*I did*, I'd say. *He said it's normal. It'll go up and then go down. You be on top of it. I'll be late today.*

I'd check again, skin hot as coal. And I'd think of calling, but I wouldn't.

I don't want to be one of those mothers.

I'd put it down. When I'd return, it would be cold, too cold.

For a second, I'd think it was dead.

And worse, my first feeling wouldn't be panic. It would be relief.

Then it would cry. Alive. I'd hate myself. But not enough. If it had died, you'd have blamed me, said, *you never wanted to be a mother.* And I'd have sobbed, choking, because it's true, and not true. I would've wanted it. I would've. And still, I'd wish it gone. But for now, it's here, and we are here too; and we'd touch it for proof, fight over its temperature, and exhaust ourselves into silence. Busy purposeful, saved for the time being by the tyranny of diapers and milk.

Then, one day, I'd snap, leave a note, careless, a scrap of paper folded by the crib. No goodbyes. And I'd walk out. Vanish. Cheap. Dull. Broken into silence.

Except, I wouldn't do that. Not really. I'd stay.

The betrayal comes dressed in pink. Ice cream. Strawberry. You said it so casually, like it was nothing; like eight years of chocolate meant jack shit. Even the cashier at Baskin flinched. Eight years of bitter, dark communion ending with sex and silence. Eight years of fucking smeared with chocolate's bite. And you said *strawberry*.

Straw—fucking—berry.

Strawberry is what others eat. Strawberry is compromise in a cup. It's soft, whorish, and pink in all the wrong places. It doesn't bite back. And you, spoon in hand, lips sticky, turn to me and ask, *do you want some?* And I, loyal bitch, say, *sure*.

But not tonight. *Drink number eight nine.* I don't know. Repeat.

And we kiss, my mouth stuffed with strawberry tongue until I gag on the counterfeit of you. You taste like Digene. Like pink chalk. Like the ghost of desire. And we go home. Fuck. Maybe. *Happy?* you ask. And I nod. Say *sure*.

You'll drag up the door slam. Boom. Echo. Myth. Then you'll say you don't care. Doesn't matter. Let it go. But you'll bring it up.

One of us had to do it—bolt for the exit, light the fuse, sooner later tonight tomorrow. One of us had to flee. Escape? Doesn't feel like escape. Drift, maybe. A trial run.

And if you want me back, come. Just come. Get in the car and drag me back if you must. Thirteen missed calls. *Darling.* I let them be. *Why don't you come back?* you'll ask. Like it's that simple. Like I didn't take the car. Which I did.

*I can't*, I want to say. Plus, I am stuck here, waiting for … fries. Peri-peri. The ones you like. Cute. Leave me alone, get out of my head, leave leave leave now fuck off please. But how long will you last …? How long before the bartender says *last orders*? How long before I have to choose: Drive drunk or sleep nowhere? Because I can't be stuck for the night. Why not. Because I can't. And because they have to shut. Everything shuts. And look—there is only so much stuck we're allowed per life, and I burnt through my quota a long time ago. You get one or the other. Stuck or dead.

So, I get unstuck. Maybe I'll call you, ask for the card we buried for apocalypse. Well, newsflash, here it is. But you won't answer. You'll say, *thirteen times I called*.

13–1. I call again. 13–2. Shit. I hate myself for keeping count, but I know you're doing it too. Math and misery. And you have the advantage. I know. You know. *She doesn't have enough to check into a hotel.* So, for now, I sit, sweat stuck to plastic. And you sit, safe at home, maybe chewing your comfort burger, ketchup dripping down your sleeve. I haven't eaten. I'm waiting. Still. For your kind of fries. For you. For something that won't arrive. I call again. Just one ring. Hang up. But it counts. 13–3. Fuck. And in the static of waiting comes that thought again: thin, buzzy at the base of my skull. A baby. A distraction. Something soft to chain us together, to bury the silence, and stitch us shut for another year, maybe two. Then what? Who knows. Maybe fries. Maybe not. Maybe just more unanswered calls.

And then your text. *Come home.* Two words. No punctuation. Just a command. Like I'm some mutt you can whistle back. I stare at the glow, blue, thumb trembling, head full of rum and static. I type. Delete. Type again. Send. *Home stopped feeling like home a long time ago.* You read it. But send nothing back. Blue ticks stacked. That's us now. Blue ticks and silence, bloated and rancid. Why didn't you stop me? Why didn't you say something, anything? *Don't go. Fuck you. I hate you. Eat shit.* But you said nothing. You let me go. And that's the part that stings. Because you used to stop me. And now I sit, stuck on this cheap stool, bartender already scrubbing the night down, and I think about the times you chased me.

You remember? Monsoon night, me barefoot in the rain, bag half-packed, screaming down three flights. You, boxers plastered wet to your ass, yelling *come back, at least take your shoes*. Or that night, on the road, headlights burning my face, me spitting *I'm done*, and you jerking the car into a car park, yanking my wrist so hard it went purple. *Not with me*, you growled, and we kissed, violent stupid, holy.

Back then, your voice cracked when I cried. Back then, you had fight.

But tonight? Nothing. Just silence and this fucking text. *Come home.*

Madam. Your fries. Peri-peri. Thank you. And I grab one, and put it in my mouth, chew, and wash it down with Old Monk, and the bartender turns to me, last orders. Get two. Repeat. Always repeat. *Why'd you leave?* Maybe I needed to see if you'd still come after me. Maybe I needed proof of what I already knew. That, this time, you wouldn't. And now, Bar-Bar. Hindi for repeat. A coincidence? There are no accidents, you'd say, quoting that animated film. Idiot turtle. Idiot panda. Idiot me. We sat through it a dozen times, you dissecting noodles and destiny, and why'd he fall out of the sky, you'd ask, and then spend hours, a man possessed. And sure enough, YouTube delivered sermons on fate and fireworks. How many Sunday afternoons I wasted, nodding, saying *sure, hmm-hmm,* through *Transformers*, *Rocky*, *James Bond*, *Fast & Furious*, *House of Cards*, *Breaking Bad*, *Mad Men*, and that five-hour gore fest you call cinema at its finest, *Gangs of Wasseypur*. *You know,*

*Scorsese liked it. He even wrote to Kashyap.* As if that baptized it into truth. I wanted to rip your lips off with my teeth. Instead, I swallowed. Always swallowed. Revenge.

We get it. 320 minutes to kill the guy. I sat through it five times. Five. That's what you did to me. You tricked me.

My phone buzzes. Same thing. *Come home.* I call. You don't answer. 13–4. Fuck it.

And then, WhatsApp. You flirted with that girl from your office / Not this again, please / Why not, I know you did / Fuck it, let's do this / You kissed another guy, then called it a test / Said you were drunk, it didn't mean anything / You left me stranded outside the hospital that night / Phone dead, blood between my legs / Then said you were tired, fucking tired, to pick up your wife / You smashed my phone / Three months' salary gone / Laughed like it was a joke / And how convenient—now I'm your wife, other times don't call me that, I hate that label / You lied about where you were, whole nights, said it was work / For fuck's sake / You spent my birthday drunk, puking in the sink, my mother's sink / Then cried, I didn't want it to be like this / You locked me out, made me sleep in the car, two degrees, no blanket / Then texted: cool off / You made me buy plants for the balcony, said let's make it feel like home / Five times, killed them, like everything you touch, like me / You made me give up my friends, bitched until I stopped calling / You made me change my number, too many people text you, you said / You read my journals, called it drama / You made me want to kill myself, then said don't be crazy / You told me I was too loud / Well, your mother agrees / You said I was too clingy / Then panicked when I didn't answer for an hour / I'm calling again, pick up / You kept score like it was a game / You made me miss funerals, birthdays, weddings, life, because you needed me / Let's not do this, I am begging you / You made fun of my period / That was a joke, and you laughed too / You came inside me without asking, twice, said it felt more intimate / Then googled how to say I'm sorry with flowers, but never said it / You forgot our anniversary, said it's just a date, but remembered your ex's birthday / Wrote her a fucking poem, I saw it, she didn't even reply, loser / You played music I hated just to piss me off / Left dishes in the sink for days / You hit me / You too / You called me Babe, like it meant anything, like I was a placeholder for the real thing / I should've left a long time ago / Me too / You never saw me, not really / I'm calling again, pick up / Seriously. 13–5.

You call. I let it ring. 14–5.

And I need to pee. Not poetic. Not some dainty feminine urge. Just pee. So, I push myself off the sticky barstool, legs jelly, knees gone AWOL, body high on rum, the kind that drips slow into your spine, turns your bones into soup. And you catch my arm as I stumble, pretend it's chivalry and not control. *I got this*, you say, like my body's your fucking problem to solve. It's not. Not any more. Not tonight. First date memory. Fuck off.

The bathroom mirror's cracked. Not dramatic. Just a lazy diagonal through the middle, a quiet divorce no one talks about. I look in. One eye bloodshot, the other dead. A face split clean down the lie. And I sit on the toilet, jeans to knees, wall to skull, breathing through my mouth because someone before me painted the air with biryani regret. The smell is war, thick and slow. My palms are glue. My thighs are goose-pimpled. My brain is floaty, like someone detached it for maintenance and forgot to plug it back in. I check my phone. *Pick up*. Then nothing. Blue ticks. I stare at the words like they owe me something. I think of replying: *I'm done.* Out loud. Like an exorcism. Done. Finished. Finito, you smug prick. And I picture walking out of here, into the street, into some kind of air, clean or not, doesn't matter, calling a cab, packing a bag, a single bag, starting over. But where? Where will I go, to whom, what version of myself would even open the door? And then I spiral. Fast. Dirty. But why do I have to leave? You leave. But you won't. You just sit there. Crying. And everything shifts. So, I leave. And you move on before I do, and I go mad, asking, *did I do the right thing?* I am forty-four. And I hate this part. Starting over. Honest part. Pathetic part. Shit. Because despite everything, the yelling, the silence, the dead plants, the spit-flecked fights, the violence, you loved me. At my worst. Didn't you? And now my phone's in my hand again, and I see the message I sent that old friend, the one who suggested I should divorce you. Fucking bitch. I delete the chat and block her. And somewhere between sips, I check his profile. Of the one who said he loved me; the one with the wife, the dog, the Sunday sunlight on a balcony. It makes me want to throw up, yes.

Because I want it. The picture-perfect life.

And I type: *darling, let's have a baby.*

Yeah. Those words. All lowercase. No drama. No heart emoji. Just desperation. A plea. I stare at it. It looks fake. Looks like it came from someone else's life. Like maybe from a braver woman. Or a dumber one. But I know it'll work. Plus, your mother will love it.

I hit send.

Blue ticks. Seen. And there it is. No backsies. Maybe the worst decision I've ever made. Or maybe the only thing keeping me from slipping down the drain with the mop water.

Either way, I flush. Wipe my face. Zip up. The mirror catches me again. The crack runs right through my mouth. Of course it fucking does. Perfect.

The phone rings. This time, I answer. No hesitation. Just instinct. A soft, breathless hello. Your voice is warm, restrained, a little scared too, maybe, or maybe that's just me projecting hope into the pauses. *Where are you*, you ask, and I say it. *Bar-Bar. Still*. And then comes the pause, that goddamn pause where I think you'll ruin it, say something cruel or careless, something that makes all this hurt loop back into rage. But you don't. You say, *stay there. Send me the location. I'm coming to get you*. Soft. Simple. No conditions. No reproach. Not even a sigh. And my throat closes. Something breaks. Or heals. *Okay*. It sounds small. And it's stupid, how happy I am. And how immediate it is. The rush of warmth. Like I've just been cast in a film titled *The Wife Who Was Worth Coming Back For*.

And I feel chosen. Not tolerated. Not managed.

And we're going to have a baby. That's the act now. A fucking punchline with a crib. I say it to myself, a mantra, a sedative—we're going to have a baby we're going to have a baby we're going to have a baby. I don't know if it's joy or surrender. Doesn't matter. Both are heavy. Both taste like rust. *My husband's coming to get me*, I say to the bartender. Like that means anything. Like that's a goddamn medal. He nods. Doesn't look up. Doesn't care. He's been watching this scene for years. I finish the drink. *Can you pack these*, I say, *the peri-peri fries? And give me the bill*. And I sit. And I wait. I wait like a woman who has finally given up the fight. Surrendered. And that's what it is, isn't it? Giving in. Not just to him. But to everything. To the story. To the structure. Get married. Have a baby. Die. That's it. That's the whole fucking arc. There's no magic. No wild destiny. No reinvention at forty or forty-four. Just this long, slow dilution of the self into someone else's need. Funny. I thought I was immune. I thought I'd clawed my way out. That I was better. Smarter. Fuck that. I just had better lipstick and a few more orgasms. In the end, I'm still here. Sitting in a bar. Waiting for a man. Pregnant with nothing but the idea of being needed. And maybe that's all it ever was. Not love. Just fatigue. Just the long road of fuck-it paved with good intentions. And maybe that's what we mean by adulthood—choosing the cage with the softest bars. Maybe that's the secret no one tells you—we don't grow up, we just give in. One by one. With a smile that says, *let's have a baby*, even when we're not sure.

And so, I wait—wait for you to walk in and make it official. To seal the deal. To carry me back into the story I once said I'd never live. And when you come, I know I'll fold into you. Let you take me home. Let you press your lips to my hair and whisper *Ssh … relax. I got this. I got you*. And I'll believe you. Press your hand to my empty stomach and pretend it's a promise. I'll tell myself it's love. That this is a choice. That this is what grown women do. We trade our fight for furniture. Our fire for formula. And we say thank you, when we mean fuck you.

And when people ask, later, much later, how we made it, how we found our way back, how we stayed; I'll smile. I'll nod. I'll say *we worked at it*. And they'll clap. And maybe I'll even believe it. Be proud of us. Because believing is easier than burning it all down. Because you don't get medals for escape. Just ash and a couch you can't afford. And I'll love you again, find ways, new ways. Softer. Quieter. Conditional. Or maybe I won't. But either way, I'll survive. And it won't matter. Because the story will be intact. The ending will still arrive. And they will say: We did it right. We were brave. We made it. We chose each other. And I will sit in our home, beside our child, and I will say *thank you*. I will say *I'm lucky*. I will say *I'm happy*. And isn't that what love means anyway?

Not joy. Not magic. Just survival dressed in pink.

So, I wait. Not for you. But for the lie I've finally agreed to live. And when it arrives, and it will, I'll call it my happily ever after.

# ACKNOWLEDGEMENTS

My thanks to a few people without whom *happily ever after* would simply not have happened.

Neale Murray, my former boss and a dear friend, first introduced me to Jeet Thayil, opening a door that changed the course of things for me. Jeet, along with Anil Kably, went on to do something even more generous—they put me on stage at a literature festival, long before I felt I had any business being there. An act of faith that still humbles me. Jeet later offered me the chance to write *happily ever after*.

I also owe a special thanks to Dharini Bhaskar, whose patience, feedback and editorial care helped shape the piece into what it is now. Her generosity with her time and attention made the process not just better, but kinder.

I'm grateful to all of them for the encouragement, trust and quiet belief that carried this piece into being.

# ABOUT THE AUTHOR

Kamal Trilok Singh is a writer. *happily ever after* is his debut novel.